HAY HOUSE BASICS

TANTRA

TANTRA

Discover the Path from
Sex to Spirit

SHASHI SOLLUNA

HAY HOUSE

Carlsbad, California • New York City • London
Sydney •Johannesburg • Vancouver • New Delhi

First published and distributed in the United Kingdom by:
Hay House UK Ltd, Astley House, 33 Notting Hill Gate, London W11 3JQ
Tel: +44 (0)20 3675 2450; Fax: +44 (0)20 3675 2451; www.hayhouse.co.uk

Published and distributed in the United States of America by:
Hay House Inc., PO Box 5100, Carlsbad, CA 92018-5100
Tel: (1) 760 431 7695 or (800) 654 5126; Fax: (1) 760 431 6948 or (800) 650 5115
www.hayhouse.com

Published and distributed in Australia by:
Hay House Australia Ltd, 18/36 Ralph St, Alexandria NSW 2015
Tel: (61) 2 9669 4299; Fax: (61) 2 9669 4144; www.hayhouse.com.au

Published and distributed in the Republic of South Africa by:
Hay House SA (Pty) Ltd, PO Box 990, Witkoppen 2068
info@hayhouse.co.za; www.hayhouse.co.za

Published and distributed in India by:
Hay House Publishers India, Muskaan Complex, Plot No.3, B-2,
Vasant Kunj, New Delhi 110 070
Tel: (91) 11 4176 1620; Fax: (91) 11 4176 1630; www.hayhouse.co.in

Distributed in Canada by:
Raincoast Books, 2440 Viking Way, Richmond, B.C. V6V 1N2
Tel: (1) 604 448 7100; Fax: (1) 604 270 7161; www.raincoast.com

Text © Shashi Solluna, 2016

The moral rights of the author have been asserted.

Permission to use the 'belly to belly' practice on
page 119 kindly granted by David Cates.

A catalogue record for this book is available from the British Library.

ISBN: 978-1-78180-710-1

Interior illustrations: 53 Thinkstock.co.uk/MVorobiev;
179 Shutterstock.com/D. Czarnota

Printed and bound in Great Britain by TJ International Ltd, Padstow

I would like to dedicate this book to Shiva, the Highest Consciousness that has led me through life like an ever-guiding flame calling me higher and higher. Om Nama Shivaya! And to Shakti, the eternal life force that has made this life so beautiful. She is the force that reveals the mystery, the aliveness of nature, and the energy that has kept me dancing. Jai Ma!

And to the men in my life who have been a Shiva to my Shakti.

And to my earthly parents... the Shiva and Shakti known as Mum and Dad! Thank you for always supporting me to do 'whatever makes you happy'. Thank you for giving me a loving and stable foundation from which I could fly high.

Contents

Exercises and Practices   ix

Introduction   xi

PART I: ENTERING THE WORLD OF TANTRA

Chapter 1: What Can Tantra Bring to You?   3

Chapter 2: The History of Tantra   11

Chapter 3: Finding the Right Tantra for You   21

Chapter 4: Developing a Tantric Daily Practice   31

PART II: THE CORE PRINCIPLES OF TANTRA

Chapter 5: Principle 1: Everything is Sacred   51

Chapter 6: Principle 2: Desire is a Path to the Divine   61

Chapter 7: Principle 3: Use Polarity to Attain Unity   67

Chapter 8: Principle 4: Sublimate Sexual Energy   87

Chapter 9: Principle 5: Transfiguration   95

Chapter 10: The Principles of Tantric Healing   101

PART III: THE TANTRIC JOURNEY

Chapter 11: Opening Your Heart   113

Chapter 12: Sexual Healing   123

Chapter 13: Awakening Sexual Energy   143

Chapter 14: Awakening Full-body Energy   153

Chapter 15: The Art of Tantric Orgasm   183

Chapter 16: The Conscious Relationship   193

Chapter 17: Moving from Karma to Dharma   221

Conclusion: How Could Tantra Serve the World?   233

Bibliography and Recommended Reading   237

Resources   241

About the Author   245

Exercises and Practices

Exercises

Are your experiences leaving you empty?   6

Gestalt Therapy for the inner union   73

Shiva-Shakti scale   76

Playing with polarity   79

Choosing supportive friends, lovers and communities   117

Healing shadow desires   126

Understanding the messages   128

How is your energy?   158

What kind of lover are you?   175

Your current relationship status   195

Practices

Innocent intimacy meditation   8

Tantric breath meditations   35

Tandava 45

Offering to the Divine 55

Eye-gazing 57

Circle of light 80

Sublimating emotions 92

Transfiguration 98

Listening to your heart 115

Atisha's Heart Meditation for self-love 119

Taoist 'Inner Smile' meditation 131

Genital sun bath 134

Genital revelation 135

Shakti meditation 145

Shakti sounding 148

Sexual energy awakening 150

Five-element massage 172

Self-pleasuring meditation 189

Simple prayers 205

Belly to belly – embodied intimacy 213

Sex magic – raising energy with intention 224

Introduction

'The Tantric way is open to all the richness of human nature, which it accepts without a single restriction.'

DANIEL ODIER

Tantra is often defined as 'to weave', and can be compared to weaving fabric. Tantra is therefore a path that weaves together. But what exactly is it that is being woven and why?

We experience a lot of pain when we feel a split in our lives. Whenever we feel torn two ways we feel an inner conflict, and it can also manifest as outer conflict too. Often we don't even realize that our challenges in life are due to this underlying split. For example, we may think and say that we want a relationship, but inside we fear commitment and can't understand why we aren't attracting a stable relationship. Or maybe you know you are torn, and suffer: part of you wants a stable job and structure, and another part wants to travel free.

Tantra is about merging. It is about uniting. It is about making love.

Tantra is about uniting all that has become split apart – creating wholeness, healing and totality – so at last your life can flow with ease and with a sense of 'choicelessness'. There is one way, one truth. Life becomes a river that you can flow along with, rather than a complex planning strategy, a confusing chaos or a painful battlefield.

One of the big places in which our lives can be divided is between everyday life and spiritual reality. In the metaphysics of Tantra, however, the world can be understood to have two dimensions: horizontal and vertical.

The horizontal dimension is the world we see around us: our friends, family, relationships and experiences. The objects we handle on a daily basis, the physical location where we live, and so on. For most people this is reality.

The vertical dimension is the pole that runs between heaven and earth and is, in general, much less familiar. This aspect of reality highlights that we can, at times, experience a very physical solid reality – bodies, objects, etc. – but at other times we experience a much less tangible universe – thoughts, emotions, energies and even states of consciousness. Think of a time you felt extreme joy or ecstasy and felt as though you were being lifted into the skies – this is the lift upwards in the vertical reality.

Tantra 101

Horizontal reality: The life around you – your relationships, your surroundings and your experiences.

Vertical reality: Life between the solid physical level of awareness and higher states of expanded consciousness.

Ultimately, Tantra points us to the highest level of consciousness in which we merge into what is often called 'oneness', in which we no longer feel like a separate physical entity. This is sometimes called 'heaven', as opposed to the more tangible experience of 'earth' (physical reality). In Tantra, orgasm is one of the key ways to move from a physical solid experience of reality into the lighter more ethereal experience. In other words, orgasm can take us from earth to heaven.

However Tantra also invites us onto the path of creativity, in which we bring the heavenly vibrations back down into this earthly experience. A lot of music, poetry and dance are examples of this. In Tantra you can also channel the divine into your touch, and give healing or loving to another person through your body. So Tantra invites us to move from sex to spirit and from spirit to sex as a creative dance of life.

Now this can be quite startling, if you were raised with any conventional religion, as most of the world's religions give the message that sexuality is a non-spiritual phenomenon, or even anti-spiritual; at best used to create babies and at worst a vehicle to take you to damnation and hell. Tantra does not teach that *all* sexual experiences take you to higher consciousness, but it does give step-by-step guidance to help put you on the path to sacred sexuality.

This metaphysical theory also explains why Tantra is so often the 'black sheep' of spiritual systems. On many spiritual and religious paths we are faced with a choice: sexuality OR spirituality. Tantra gives a different invitation: choose sexuality AND spirituality, and bring the two together to create a wholeness and completion within your life. This is the weaving of Tantra.

So Tantra is a path that unites apparent opposites into totality or oneness, including:

❖ Sexuality with spirituality

❖ Masculine with feminine

❖ Playfulness with depth

❖ Dark, shadowy parts of ourselves with the light of conscious awareness

❖ Relaxation with stimulation

❖ Meditation with experience

In fact the list is inexhaustible, as Tantra invites any apparently separate aspects of life to be brought together in union.

The catalyst for this union is love.

The path of worshipping the Divine Feminine

As you enter the world of Tantra, you will find a balance and union of opposites. Yet, in spite of this, some definitions of Tantra are actually about honouring the feminine aspect. Pandit Rajmani Tigunait, author of *Tantra Unveiled*, was the son of a practising Tantric in India. When he asked his father what Tantra was, he usually received this reply, 'Tantra means worshipping the Divine Mother. Tantrics are her blessed children. Whatever they have is by the grace of the Divine Mother.'

Does this mean that Tantra has a female deity in place of the usual masculine God? It is not so simple, although there are Tantric lineages that make rituals to feminine deities, and the famous Mahavidyas – the 10 goddesses of Adi Parashakti in Hinduism, often worshipped in classical Tantric practice (*see also page 180*).

However, Tantra is not about replacing the idea of a man on a cloud with a long white beard with a woman on a cloud with long flowing hair! In fact, once you start delving into Tantra, you'll discover that it has a unique way of honouring the energy of life, and finding the divine within it. This energy is *Shakti* and its divine vibration within each human is called 'Kundalini Shakti'.

Tantra 101

Sexual energy is generally referred to as Shakti, though this term can be very broad and include anything that is part of life! There is a specific Shakti of each element: a water Shakti, a fire Shakti and so on.

Kundalini Shakti, or just kundalini, is a more specific term to refer to the stream of creative life force that runs through each individual (*see also page 40*). It may be dormant, but once awakened it brings an animation to a person that might be called spirited. If we say a person has a lot of spirit, we may be seeing their kundalini. It is so alive that it is often described as an 'intelligence'. Some see this energy as the Goddess, though it can also animate a man's body so this can be confusing. One way or another, it is seen as a living manifestation of God or Consciousness.

So rather than looking for the divine beyond life, we look *within* life – within energy. When you walk in lush nature you may feel this divine presence, as many people feel interconnected to all that is when they are in the natural world. Tantrics would say this sense of oneness is due to the flow of Shakti energy. If you were to sit in a park of plastic plants, you wouldn't feel that same presence because this divine energy comes from living things.

So while the ascetic lives out of the flow of life – perhaps in a cave, desert or monastery – and abstains from sensual pleasures and relationships in order to find God. The Tantric path goes *into* the flow of life to find God, through the Goddess. The Goddess is the flow of life force and the God is the source of that flow. The Goddess is the divine manifest and the God is the divine unmanifest.

So the worship of the Divine Feminine is about finding pure flows of energy and honouring them. Not all of life is made of this pure flow, as much of what we experience is distorted. If it doesn't feel like love, then it is probably distorted energy! So as we worship and honour the pure flow, we awaken that pure flow within us.

> *The Tantric path is a path of healing those distorted places and freeing the pure life-force energy so that we become pure manifestations of our true divine Self.*

Some Tantrics like to do that by personifying the Divine Feminine as a Goddess or the Divine Mother, while others like to work more with energy flow. Both ways will lead to the same result: an awakening of the life-force energy; to become an interconnected part of all that is through the network of energy in this universe; to become embodiments of the Divine.

Tantra 101

Any system or teacher that abuses the feminine aspect in any way cannot be truly called 'Tantric', as it would be violating this core principle. We live in a world that often tries to own, possess and control the feminine aspect, and this aspect needs to be healed in order to enter Tantra. This distortion could take many forms including: coercing women into sex, taking advantage of someone when they are vulnerable (male or female: vulnerability is the 'feminine' side of all of us), violating the Earth's resources on our path and so on. To heal this is to move from trying to have power over the feminine into a place of honouring the feminine. This is not just about women, but the feminine aspect in all of us. It is about holding space for vulnerability, so that we can open up without harm.

The path of love

An open heart is the essential requirement for union to occur and for this reason Tantra is often described as the 'path of love' or 'the way of the heart'. Take Tantric techniques and use them without love, and the Tantra is gone.

An open heart is essential for the unification of opposites. It is the alchemical basis for healing to occur. In Tantra there are meditations and practices to help open the heart (*see page 113*) and create a space wide enough, vast enough, to allow both sides of duality to coexist. Anything that has felt split, cut off, separate or in conflict can heal in the space of the open heart.

Tantric texts

Tantra is also used to mean 'doctrine', 'framework' or 'system', and thus can be used to refer directly to the texts written in the original Tantric systems. These texts are often a conversation between the Hindu god Shiva and the goddess Shakti. They are embodiments of consciousness and energy. The paradox, however, is that these two can actually never be separated. Just as we cannot separate the meaning from the word, consciousness and energy are one; formlessness and form are one. So the texts use a kind of dualism that points back to non-dualism. In this way, Tantra helps us to grasp the paradox of life.

I am not offering Tantra here as an academic, and there are several good books that can do this (*see Bibliography and Recommended Reading, page 237*), rather as one who has found both spiritual revelation and harmony in life through my journey of the many different facets and teachings of Tantra. I wish to share what has been enlightening and healing for me, in the hope that it may also support you in your journey of life, as well as an understanding of the term Tantra and its core principles, including:

❖ An outline of the history of Tantra.

❖ The types of Tantra and Tantric practice.

❖ An understanding of the Tantric approach to sexuality.

❖ Practices to explore your own Tantric sexuality.

❖   Practices to explore Tantric sexuality with a partner.

❖   Practices to guide Tantric energetic awakening.

❖   A Tantric understanding of relationship, love and intimacy.

❖   Practices to open your heart.

❖   Practices to open your heart with your partner.

❖   An understanding of Tantra as a spiritual path.

❖   Practices for creating spiritual experiences and higher states of consciousness.

Like Tantra itself, this book will take you on a journey: back in time to the history and myths of a Tantra past; within to find your rich inner world; along the river of energy flow, releasing some blocks along the way and becoming fully alive again; and into higher states of consciousness. Along the way you will discover who you really are within and then share it with a beloved if you so choose. And you will learn how to open up to love, the love that is the expression and manifestation of your true nature.

Tantra 101

Throughout the book, you'll find practical exercises and you might find it helpful to keep a notebook or journal handy to write down any thoughts or your answers to the questions. There is something alchemical that happens when we write things down rather than simply doing them in our head.

To support your journey even deeper, you may also like to use the audio meditations accompanying this book, which you can download at ShashiSolluna.com/Tantric-Tools

As you can see, Tantra is more than a set of practices, it is a set of experiences, and your journey will be different from mine but by sharing the path I have taken so far, I hope that you will begin to sense what Tantra can bring to our lives.

My journey into Tantra

I entered into spirituality at an unusually early age, which was in part due to having an early mid-life crisis. Aged 17 I found myself drinking alcohol into oblivion on a regular basis and, though apparently having a good time (or so my friends told me!), I was missing out on my life. Waking up on my 18th birthday with a killer hangover to discover that I had been sick all over my bed (*urgh*!), I decided to find a new way of living my life.

Ironically, the day it became legal to drink I was already replete with it, and true to my word I haven't got drunk since that day. Finishing school in a daze, I had somehow managed to gain a place at Oxford University but first I headed off to India to spend a gap year working in an orphanage and so left my 'privileged', alcohol-drenched life behind for a while.

Having gone rather piously to help 'poor' orphans, I was astounded to discover some of the happiest children I had ever seen. With little more to play with than a plastic bag and a piece of string (one child would run along pulling the bag on the string and the others would chase behind trying to catch it), I found children who laughed and sang and danced, rather than whingeing for the latest computer game or designer trainers.

But what they had that touched me the most was a daily spiritual practice. There was a small temple room in the orphanage and one of the caregivers would go each day to leave offerings and chant. Sometimes we would light a big fire in the back garden and sing, dance and chant under the stars. Many special holidays were honoured with big rituals or fasting. I had found a sense of meaningfulness, making life feel special, making life sacred.

I returned to the UK and embarked on my degree in Experimental Psychology with renewed vigour. Something had touched my heart in India and I no longer wanted to lose myself in drunken university nights. I joined the yoga society, learnt meditation and became a Buddhist – chanting twice a day to an altar in my room. All the while I was also studying the effects of meditation and chanting on the brain and nervous system in my degree course. Not that it was all pious spiritual time... socially I moved away from getting drunk to discover the dance floor. Through dancing I felt an aliveness I had never felt before.

In search of totality

By 21, I had a degree and a spiritual life but in a number of areas of my life I still didn't feel whole and complete.

I was spiritual and was nourished by joining with other people in chanting circles and meditation groups, but my partying and dance spirit was also growing. I felt torn between partying and being a more spiritual person. Most of my spiritual friends were too serious to dance, and most of my party friends thought spirituality was weird.

I was also too young to be a Buddhist nun, yet too spiritual to be entirely satisfied with love and sexuality the way it was presented in my social circles. I'd had a long-term relationship through my university years, but my boyfriend was totally disinterested in my spiritual side. For me, living together and having occasional sex with the lights out wasn't nourishing my soul. I loved him, but the relationship wasn't in alignment with my deepest spiritual calling. I felt split.

I chose the spiritual part of my life, as it felt most meaningful, broke off our engagement and headed off to India again on a spiritual quest to find teachers, gurus and guides, to visit spiritual sites, to meditate, to chant, to live in caves and sleep in hammocks on the beach, and generally immerse myself in my spiritual journey.

Whilst on my journey, the millennium happened. I found myself in Goa with some of my college friends, dressed in costumes and going to all-night raves full of colour and crazy hippies and psychedelic experiences. My party self was fulfilled but my spiritual self was overwhelmed! More often than not I'd end up sitting on a hill overlooking the party, chanting Buddhist mantras as the sun was rising. I still felt torn who to be, where to go.

Then I found Osho. More precisely I found the Osho Ashram, as the teacher Osho had actually left his body 10 years before I reached his Ashram (now called a 'meditation resort'). The first 'meditation' I joined was a heart-dance in which we moved around singing heart-opening songs while looking into the eyes of strangers. The second meditation was dancing wildly to live drums. No drugs, no alcohol, no confused party-frenzy... just dancing!

It was a ground-breaking moment in my life – my spiritual self and my party self finally united as one! No more splitting apart or yo-yoing from one to the other. Finally they met and merged. My heart felt as if it had cracked open and soared to the skies, as I danced with all of these amazing people. Though they lost themselves in dancing, their consciousness was not lost along the way as seemed to happen at raves. These people were present, completely present, with their ecstasy. A natural ecstasy that Osho always said was our birthright.

The other uniting thing that began to happen, although at a gentler pace, was my sexual self and my spiritual self. My spiritual self had become rather like a celibate monk. I was spiritual, but at the cost of my juiciness. I was dry and serious. Heading towards enlightenment, but definitely not enlivened!

At the Osho Ashram I began to hear about Tantra. Osho was a key person in bringing this ancient spiritual path back to life again, and bringing it to Westerners. He often talked of Tantra being the path that unites opposites together: exactly the experience I had had when I first entered his ashram. The result?

Osho called Tantra 'totality':
to feel whole and complete, to be free of
inner conflicts and contradictions.

I longed for that.

Tantra and sex

Tantra always stands out from other spiritual paths, as it is, perhaps, the one most people are both intrigued and intimidated by. I was no exception. I knew that the ashram had Tantra workshops, but I was no way near ready to take the risk of joining one. What if I had to take off all my clothes? What if there was an orgy? All of my Tantra projections arose in full. I watched the women who were into Tantra floating around the ashram in their sexy dresses, decadent jewellery and sashaying hips. At first I judged them as being completely unspiritual. Yet another part of me was just longing to be as beautiful as they were.

Like many women, I grew up with that persistent model of dualistic female models: virgin versus whore, nun versus temptress, mother versus sexual freedom. It was an impossible choice. In my world you couldn't integrate both: you had to choose. You were either the good girl with limited sex drive and monogamous long-term relationship or you were the rebel, living wild and free – but at the price of being rejected by society and having to give up your motherly, loving and spiritual qualities. No wonder I was experiencing such inner conflict.

Yet now, I was watching women who were spiritual and sexy at the same time. These were women who meditated daily, who listened to discourses on enlightenment, who wore robes and sat in silence. These were women who danced wild and free, lived with open hearts, had juicy love affairs yet loved deeply, and experienced mind-blowing, all-night lovemaking. I was intrigued. I wanted to enter this world somehow...

And then I fell in love.

I met a man from the ashram whom I immediately recognized as a soul mate. We really didn't take too much time to hold back... very soon we had fallen deeply in love, moved in together and merged the two rivers of our lives into one. I was to stay with him for nine years and in that time I entered the wonderful world of Tantra. Finally my spiritual life and my intimate life merged into one. I was on the path to totality and wholeness at last.

The next 15 years were an unexpected journey into Tantra. Unexpected because there is really no way to comprehend what Tantra will bring you until you experience it. Tantra is very much an experiential path that cannot be grasped by a mental understanding alone. Tantra is a path through practice and relating to life to taste what lies behind life. We can read books about Tantra (such as this one) for inspiration, but at the end of the day to know Tantra we need to experience it.

Having said all of that, it is possible to read and understand the principles underlying Tantra, the practices and meditations, and some of the poetry of the ancient texts. Reading about Tantra can help demystify the topic, ease any concerns and empower you to choose the right teacher and course for you. It may also inspire you to develop a Tantra practice, whether alone or with a loved one.

Part I

ENTERING THE WORLD OF TANTRA

'Our purpose in this life is to live in higher consciousness and to teach others to live in higher consciousness.'

Yogi Bhajan

Chapter 1

What Can Tantra Bring to You?

*'The original Tantrik worldview: a way of seeing
and understanding reality that can challenge
you to the deepest levels of your being.'*

CHRISTOPHER D. WALLIS

You may already be gaining a sense of what Tantra can bring into your life. It can bring spirituality for those who are already very sexual, but looking for more depth and meaning. It can bring sexual awakening to those who are already very spiritual, but perhaps yearn to share that spiritual experience with another in a physical way. It can bring peace to anyone who feels split between different aspects of themselves or in their lives.

Over the years I have seen people drawn to the path of Tantra for oodles of reasons. These include:

❖   To experience a richer, more fulfilling sex life.

❖   To heal a past sexual trauma.

❖   To find more meaning in sexuality.

- ❖ To overcome a fear of intimacy.

- ❖ To become more alive, radiant and free.

- ❖ To open the heart and experience more love.

- ❖ To heal and clear relationship problems.

- ❖ To reboot a relationship that feels dull.

- ❖ To discover and develop their own sexuality and sexual polarity.

- ❖ To gain understanding of the opposite sex and better skills in relating.

- ❖ To bring spiritual experiences into the physical body.

- ❖ To develop a spiritual relationship with a partner.

- ❖ To work with energy.

- ❖ To make life sacred and purposeful.

- ❖ To access spiritual experiences and elevate the state of consciousness.

- ❖ To heal inner 'splits' and inner conflicts and feel whole and complete.

- ❖ Gut instinct – simply drawn to Tantra without even knowing why.

Whether you are a couple or an individual, Tantra may have something to offer you. Whether you are seeking spiritual experience or sexual opening, Tantra brings you gifts. And as intimacy is a desire at the core of human experience, Tantra can help to lead you to a richer, more fulfilling way of life.

However, it is worth noting that while a particular desire might bring you onto the path of Tantra, it may transform into a very different form of fulfilment than you were expecting. You may come to Tantra to develop orgasmic potential, and discover a unity with all of life that you were not expecting. As a good friend of mine, Eyal Matsliah, once said:

'I came to Tantra for the sex; and I found God.'

The desire for intimacy

Even though Tantra is a spiritual path, the majority of people attending workshops and events are really looking for *intimacy*. In Tantra this isn't judged as a bad thing, as it's not necessary to pretend to be drawn to workshops *just* for a spiritual experience. Tantra is a path of desire, and in fact sees desire as a fuel for awakening, if used in the right way.

Intimacy is often something we titillate at, or feel awkward at the mere mention of, yet Tantra acknowledges a universal truism: humans have a huge desire for intimacy. Judgement around intimacy means that many people suppress their need for it or try to replace with it shopping, eating, alcohol, drugs, porn, television, social media and so on.

Yet these external things can leave us feeling empty because they can't fulfil our deep human need for connection. From the moment we pop out of the birth canal into this world, we are searching for intimacy with our mother's breast, her warmth, and the skin-to-skin contact as we drink a fluid from her body into ours. Though the form of intimacy we seek will change, as we grow older, this need for connection is a fundamental part of being a human.

Ultimately we desire to get high, to be elevated above everyday reality. We long to feel uplifted out of our sense of limiting structure and separation, and to touch the place where we feel interconnected with everything. Of course, many people reach to drugs for this experience, but these often bring you crashing down into an even more painful sense of separation than before. When we learn to raise sexual energy with full consciousness, we can get truly high, with our feet still on the earth... and share this expansion with those we are intimate with in our lives. As Margot Anand described it:

> 'I realized that existential or psychological pain was actually the absence of ecstasy. It was the outcome of being cut off from the source of one's being, the source of life.'

Exercise: Are your experiences leaving you empty?

Take a moment to consider the actions, items or substances that you desire for your pleasure. Make a list so you are aware of what they are.

❖ How conscious do you remain while engaging in them? Do you stay present with the sensations of pleasure, or do you switch off in some way? Do you find you 'leave your body'? Do you even lose consciousness, as with drugs and alcohol?

❖ Do you judge any of those behaviours, either in yourself or in others?

❖ Do you have a dual personality: one part that you show to the 'respectable' world, and another that you keep separate from it?

❖ How do you feel 'the morning after'? Do you feel at peace with yourself? Or do you experience any level of guilt, shame or regret?

❖   Do you ever seek something but once you get it are then unable to be fully present with it or to receive it fully?

Try to answer these questions honestly. It is only for your self-understanding, so there is no need to censor your answers. Notice also how you feel, as you answer them. Are there any sensations in your body? It can be useful to sit with these feelings for a few moments and even make a note of them alongside your other answers.

Innocent intimacy

Tantra introduces the concept of 'innocent intimacy' that can be healing simply by contemplating it. We so often attach layers of guilt to our core human desire for intimacy, that we judge ourselves and we judge others for having this need. Some people spend a lifetime battling against their core desires. It is a battle against life, and no one wins.

Yet Tantra offers us a return to innocence, and in the same way a baby desires their mother's breast, we may desire a hug, a caress, a kiss, getting lost in the eyes of a beloved, or dissolving into sexual union... and that all of these desires are innocent at their core.

Tantra 101

Before starting any of the practices or meditation, such as the ones given below and in the following chapters, it is very supportive to create a peaceful environment.

Find a quiet space where you won't be disturbed and switch all mobile devices to flight mode. The Internet has become one of our biggest sources of distraction, so set it aside for your practice period.

Get seated in a comfortable position. Traditionally sitting cross-legged on a cushion is known to benefit meditation. But if this is uncomfortable for you then sit on a chair. Whichever position you take make sure your spine is as straight as possible to aid your energy flow. Buddha didn't find enlightenment while slumped in a couch-potato position!

While meditating, you may prefer pure silence or the sounds of nature or soft meditation music to carry you – whatever is comfortable is fine.

How often you practise is up to you and your life. It is always advisable to do some form of practice daily after waking up, even if only for a few minutes. This is a way to tune in to the highest vibration available ready for your day. If you find a noticeable effect from any meditation or practice then repeat it daily. Use your inner shifts as your guide to what to practise and how often.

More ideas for developing your meditation practices are available on my website: ShashiSolluna.com/Tantric-Tools

Practice: Innocent intimacy meditation

This meditation can help restore our innocent intimacy, start to forgive ourselves for our desires and allow us to experience pleasure in a conscious, guilt-free way. It can also help us see beyond the object of our desires and discover the inner sensations that we are really seeking. Once we discover those within, our attachment to external objects shifts. Instead of endlessly longing for something outside of ourselves, we can start to feel fulfilled within. We move from feeling empty to feeling full, and from that fullness we can share.

1. If you could receive any kind of intimacy right now, what would it be? Would you ask for a hug, or would you most like to be held and have your hair stroked? Would you like to have sweetnothings whispered in your ear? (Don't assume you want the biggest, most dramatic thing; check in with yourself. Sometimes we automatically think we would want the elaborate four-course meal, when in truth all we want is an apple in this moment.)

2. After you have found the one simple thing you would like to receive, take a moment to close your eyes and imagine receiving it. How does it make you feel? Notice the inner sensations it brings you. Possibly you feel relaxed and melted, or perhaps stimulated and enlivened. Maybe it's that warm fuzzy feeling you desire, or the sense of being unconditionally loved and accepted.

3. Meditate on those feelings by watching them, as if they are the most fascinating things in all of existence. At this point you can drop the imagination of the outer experience (the hug, the touch, etc.), and watch the inner sensations that have been generated.

4. With your eyes still closed, notice these inner sensations in detail: what they feel like, where in your body they are, whether they rest or move. You are now getting in contact with the *energy* of the experience. You do not need to control it or try and make something happen: simply watch what is going on inside, no matter how subtle or strong it is.

5. Take deeper, fuller breaths and use the breath to make space for the inner sensations. Notice how deep breathing affects the quality of your inner sensations.

6. When you are ready to complete this meditation, place a hand over your body where the sensations feel the strongest. Simply rest the hand there for a few breaths, as if thanking the energy, thanking the sensations of your own pleasure.

7.   Open your eyes and look around: how does the world look now after a few moments of entering the sensations of your pleasure?

Tantra can bring us a sense of deep peace with the human experience, and a return to innocence. Finally we can live our lives, in these bodies, without guilt or shame. Finally we can simply be. With the guilt and self-judgement out of the way, we can get on with loving.

Loving yourself, loving others and sharing
intimacy are all natural expressions of love.

SUMMARY

✦   People enter Tantra for many reasons, from sexual healing to relationship development to spiritual seeking.

✦   Tantra is about finding the depth and meaningfulness in life.

✦   Tantra makes everyday life sacred again.

✦   Tantra can help you to come to terms with your own desires and access the energy within those desires, channelling that energy in healthy ways.

Chapter 2
The History of Tantra

*'In the scriptures you will find the way to realize
God. But after getting all the information
about the path, you must begin to work,
only then can you attain your goal.'*

SRI RAMAKRISHNA

It is always helpful when embarking on a path to know where it came from and who has walked it before. We get more of a sense of our own journey when we have a sense of history. We can also find which path is the one we are drawn to when we know a little of the lineages and different flavours of the field.

Tantra has quite a hazy history, due to the fact that the teachings were passed down by word of mouth, it was often practised in private and frequently went underground, when challenged by other religions. Additionally, Tantra was often passed on as a series of initiations from teacher to disciple, administered when the teacher felt the disciple was ready – and this still remains true today to an extent. Thus the whole field of Tantra is shrouded in mystery.

However, the earliest records of Tantra were found in India and these teachings appeared to have been carried between Tibet and China, changing form as they merged with different cultures. The earliest Taoist Sexual Arts are recorded in the *Yellow Emperor's Classic of Internal Medicine* (770–256BCE), while the earliest Tantra texts date from the seventh century. However, the teachings may predate the writings and we can understand the history of Tantra as a patchwork of different teachers, practices and communities that rose and fell throughout the ages.

The term 'Tantra' itself belongs to a set of spiritual writings, known as the *Agamas*. These often take the form of a conversation between Shiva and Shakti, the divine masculine and feminine (*see also page 70*). Authorship of these texts is not always known, some even say that Shiva was a man who existed and channelled the works and was the true founder of yoga. Others see Shiva as the divine masculine, rather than as a human embodiment. For example it is said that Shiva revealed an ancient Tantric text *The Spandakarika* to Vasugupta in the ninth century, which is most likely a poetic way to explain that he channelled this text during a high state of consciousness.

Various teachers throughout history have read and given discourse on these texts. Thus a common feature of the more classical Tantra sects is the use of Tantric texts for guidance and awakening. A particular sect may only use one text, or they may cover many.

Three major streams of influence over time have been Kashmir Shaivism, Tibetan Tantra and Taoism – although the latter is not actually considered to be a type of Tantra.

However, Taoist teachings on sexual energy, orgasm, the uniting of opposites and meditation are so closely paralleled to those in Tantra that many practitioners choose to embrace both concurrently. It may well be that the Taoist Sexual Arts were carried to India, as many teachers used to travel vast distances carrying the teachings with them, but there is no solid evidence of this.

Tantra's roots

Kashmir Shaivism is often thought of as the true root of Tantra. As the name implies, it originates from the Kashmir region. It is a very detailed spiritual path, with methods of accessing transcendent states by going deeper into life. Rather than teaching an ascetic path, Shaivism embraces life and uses its experiences to raise consciousness. You do not have to sit in a cave to enter this path, but immerse yourself deeply in life and awaken there.

The teacher and philosopher Abhinavagupta from the 10th century is perhaps one of the most renowned masters in this lineage. Abhinavagupta wrote the text known as *Tantraloka*, which endeavoured to summarize all knowledge of the Tantric texts. He himself had several gurus and was born into the Kaula lineage (his parents actually used Tantric union to conceive him). He gave many great discourses on the texts and was also known for his enlightened poetry and writings.

The practices and philosophies found within Kashmir Shaivism are so close to those found in Tibetan Buddhist Tantra that there can be no doubt of the connection between them. Obviously these traditions were carried throughout the Himalayan region. Guru Rinpoche Padmasambhava was one of the teachers that took the wisdom from India to Tibet in the eighth century and was so advanced that he was called the 'Second Buddha'.

As in many traditions, the male teachers often started schools and wrote or gave discourses on texts. Meanwhile the females were the carriers of the wisdom and passed on the Tantric wisdom via dance, music, lovemaking and art forms. We hear of Dakinis, Tantrikas and Devadasis who often lived in temples transmitting Tantric energies. In Taoism we hear of the courtesans who taught the secrets of sexual energy and longevity to the Chinese emperors.

Tantra 101

If you want to know more about women's role in Tantra's history read Miranda Shaw's excellent book *Passionate Enlightenment*, an academic review of the role of women throughout Tantra.

Sacred union

Tantra's history offers some interesting stories that tell of the meeting of a male ascetic Tantric with a wild Tantric woman and the union that resulted.

For example, one account tells of the learned Buddhist monk Saraha who lived in the eighth century. Saraha was a well-respected teacher and advisor to the king and court but one day, following a vision in a dream, he left his life to follow a Dakini, who worked as an arrow-maker in the marketplace. He saw in her the great teacher that he had been looking for his whole life. She was not academically learned but had such a deep presence when making arrows that Saraha bowed down to her.

When Saraha went to live in a cremation ground with her – dancing and singing and celebrating – the king thought he had gone mad and sent people to get him back, but each of them ended up joining the Dakini, even the king's own wife. In the end the king, too, went to follow the Dakini, and a new era of Tantric culture was born. The fruits of Saraha's experience are to be found in the beautiful texts *The Songs of Saraha*.

We see a similar pattern with several other Tibetan Tantric Masters: Naropa, Luipa, Tilopa and Marpa Lotsawa, as all of them left highly prestigious monastic lives to follow women of an untouchable caste, in order to move beyond scholastic practice and into an awakening of spontaneity. Often they lived in cremation ground, representing transcendence of cultural norms and in each case it is seen as the ultimate stage of their process. When Saraha took a Dakini as his consort he said, 'Only now am I a truly pure being.'

Not only do these stories suggest the different roles of men and women in Tantra, but also the essential union of both in order to enter the final stages of totality. When the two get together and unite, yogi and yogini, then they can enter a state of spontaneity and bliss. This difference of practice for men and women is often replicated in modern-day Tantra, and is especially seen in work around polarity.

Tantra 101

It is worth noting that in the Tibetan Buddhist stories sexual Tantric union always came after many years of solitary practice, as it was generally believed that the passions were too untamed and unconscious otherwise.

Another big name in the history of Tantra was the teacher Gorakshanath, or Gorakhnath. He was known to have been important in the Tantric lineage of practitioners called the Nath Yogis in the 11th century, which was originally founded by his teacher, a master called Matsyendra. This lineage produced the text of *Hatha Yoga Pradipika* and was an important foundation for *asana* (posture) practice that we see in modern-day yoga. In fact some forms of yoga still contain a Tantric element (working with energy), whereas others focus only on the physical postures themselves.

Different paths

Sometimes Tantra is classified into right- and left-handed paths. The right-handed path practice abstains from all sexual practices and works only with energy and meditation. The left-handed path embraces sexual activity, as well as other practices; they are also known to discard many conventional standards of morality and have rituals involving consuming meat, fish and alcohol, and engaging in sexual activity.

Just as in the Tibetan Tantric stories of ascetic monks taking consorts for the final stage of their awakening, some practitioners would follow a non-sexual path until they were ready to maintain consciousness in the midst of the strong stimulating circumstances of lovemaking. Others follow a more open and free path until they feel they have purified their desires enough to move into celibacy.

There is also the classification of red, white and black Tantra, which reflects the flavour of each school. White Tantra focuses on meditation and solo practices. Red Tantra includes optional sexual explorations and meditations with partners, and works more with the senses. Black Tantra is describing those who embrace the dark energies in life, as part of their awakening. This can be a powerful spiritual practice but Black Tantra is also known for being a path for those who misuse energy to manipulate others. This strand of practices has given Tantra a bad name, especially in India.

Sadly the suppression of sexuality in India seems to have pushed Tantra into only the extremes of black or white. You will find plenty of Tantra teachers who only use meditation, yoga, mantra and yantra, with no sexual element at all. Or you hear horrific stories of Tantric Babas that are performing rites rather like black magic. As a result, Westerners who travel to India to find Tantra to make their relationship more sacred are often confused and disappointed by what they find there.

Thus much of the Tantra you'll find in the West is rooted in Red Tantra, and it couples a desire to find happiness within relationships with sexual liberation, so perhaps then no wonder it is flourishing. Those following a White Tantra tradition may tut and look disdainfully upon the rise of Red Tantra as not being 'real', but it is worth remembering that it once existed in an India that was much more sexually liberated. We have a few temples, carvings, paintings and dance arts left as testament to these days gone by.

Tantra thus has many branches, several of which went underground or fell into decline with the invasion of the

Mughal Empire (1736–47), and with the rise to power of other religions that felt threatened by the radical practices of the Tantrics. The British colonization of India in the early 19th century was famous for bringing with it prudish Victorian attitudes and judgement towards the Tantric traditions, dancers, practitioners and texts that they found.

Therefore, it is hard to find any existing Tantric lineage that we can say is pure. Many of the practices have been absorbed into other religions such as Buddhism and Hinduism, but at the expense of their Tantric essence. Just as we see in many other world religions, when a living truth is forced into the box of dogma or fear-based ritual practices, the living truth is often destroyed in the process.

An exception to this may be the unusual path of the Baul Mystics that originated in the Bengal region of India. Disguised as travelling minstrels, the Bauls passed on teachings, as well as energy activations, through music and celebration, and so avoided suppression. There are still Baul Mystics in India to this day.

But in spite of its long history of suppression, the spirit of Tantra lives on and we are now seeing a worldwide resurgence of its traditions. Google the word 'Tantra' and you will find a wide range of teachers, practices and workshops.

There is something to be said for
such a spontaneous reawakening…
that Tantra comes alive again.

However, there is also the risk that much that uses this name bears little resemblance to the original teachings and thus weakens the use of the word. Some people randomly attach the title 'Tantra' to any sort of sexual exploration in the hope that it spiritualizes it and this may then prevent sincere seekers from finding any true spiritual benefit from it. Yet, we are experiencing history writing itself, and possibly in another 1,000 years there will be academics researching the blog posts and Facebook updates for all things 'Tantra' from this era.

Neo-Tantra

The term for modern-day Tantra, 'Neo-Tantra', has been around since the late Indian mystic Osho Rajneesh (1931–90) started to share Tantric meditations with his followers. Osho played a big part in the reintroduction of Tantra worldwide and many of today's best-known teachers are a part of his lineage.

Neo-Tantra incorporates many modern therapeutic processes with meditation and energy practices, while tending to separate itself from the classical practices (e.g. yoga, mantra and yantra meditations) although some teachers are fusing the two methodologies. Osho gave discourses from many ancient texts to his followers, and yet he also felt that modern-day practitioners needed modern-day therapy before they could even begin a meditation practice. Osho himself taught that experiential processes needed to be combined with meditation, but not all Neo-Tantra teachers reflect this, and sometimes the meditation aspect is scarce or lacking.

Today we have an abundance of teachings attributed to Tantra, which means there's plenty of choice.

The challenge is knowing which Tantric path to choose so the best way is to set an intention and then allow the path to choose you.

SUMMARY

❖ Tantra originated in India, though there are related paths found in Tibet (Dogzen) and China (Taoism).

❖ The word 'Tantra' relates to the Tantric texts, sometimes called *Tantras* or *Agamas*, and emerged from Kashmir Shaivism of which there are many different sects but which is the foundation of traditional Tantra.

❖ Guru Rinpoche Padmasambhava, the 'Second Buddha', carried the teachings to Tibet and from that originated Tibetan Tantric Buddhism and Dogzen.

❖ Taoism, a spiritual path originating in China, also carries many teachings around working with sexual energy. These practices are distinct enough from the Tantric ones to belong to a separate school. Yet the similarities mean that many practitioners are drawn to both lineages.

❖ History often shows different pathways for men and for women, with men following a monastic and scholarly path and women learning arts, music and dance. The final stage is the sexual union of two such adepts.

❖ The late mystic Osho Rajneesh played an important role in the reawakening of modern-day Tantra, which is often called Neo-Tantra.

Chapter 3

Finding the Right Tantra for You

'Synchronicity is the language of Existence', so ask the Universe, and then listen for guidance.'

PREM BABA

If you want to experience something truly Tantric it is worth setting the intention for finding a teacher who serves your highest purpose. Then trust the synchronicities that lead you to a teacher or path. Watch out for books that catch your eye, posts on social media that draw you, comments from friends – the universe is always guiding us, but it is our task to truly listen and respond.

Decide on your intention: what do you want to gain from your journey into Tantra? If you want an intellectual knowledge then you are best to seek a traditional teacher who works with the ancient texts, whereas if you want to open up more then an experiential Neo-Tantra teacher may serve your needs better. If you love yoga, then you could enter Tantric yoga as a vehicle into this field.

Tantra 101

A great way to find out what works for you is to attend one of the Tantra festivals, as you can get a taste of the many different teachers and styles of teaching available. These events happen worldwide and can provide you with the opportunity to try out a range of workshops to find the right one for you.

Conscious sexuality and Tantra

There are many teachers who can help you overcome sexual inhibitions and open up to more intimacy, but it is not Tantra unless that teacher can also help you work with meditation and energy. These are the Shiva (meditation) and Shakti (energy) principles of Tantra. The field of conscious sexuality has a lot to offer, especially on a therapeutic level. Many people who explore this for a while become naturally drawn towards Tantra.

Next you might want to think about the format. Do you need a group session or one-on-one healing? Groups are great for working through fear of expression and intimacy. But if you are carrying a lot of trauma, especially around sexuality, then it may be better to seek one-to-one healing sessions first.

Many people are drawn into Tantra to resolve a problem with their sexual life or intimacy, but later realize that the ultimate solution is a spiritual one and thus embrace the spiritual dimensions of Tantra. It doesn't matter what draws you in, but it is worth embracing Tantra's spiritual dimension from the start.

*The spiritual dimensions of Tantra can sometimes
involve trusting those who have walked before
you, inspiring you to keep up practices until
you experience these dimensions for yourself.*

Beware the shadow side

Sexual energy is very powerful and there are always some teachers that may use this power for personal gain or advantage. Sometimes in our desperation to heal, or desire for enlightenment, we may overlook a situation that in our heart of hearts we know to be out of alignment.

You never need to give away your power to another person for spiritual attainment. Spiritual awakening is only about surrendering to the Ultimate Love or God. If a teacher demands money, energy or sex in a way that doesn't feel right, stop and feel into your heart. Your heart will open and expand when a situation is right for you and contract, or move into fear, if not.

*Trust your heart, and if you are not
100 per cent sure, then do not act at all.*

Many schools place restrictions on teacher-student intimate relations to avoid misuse of power. For example, Osho (*see page 19*) had clear guidelines about intimacy for all facilitators to follow with a time period after the workshop. Not all schools follow this practice so check before you sign up for a workshop. If you are drawn to a school with more open boundaries, be sure to choose what serves your highest aims and feels good for you. What works for one person won't necessarily work for another, so look around until you find what resonates.

Different methods

If you decide to try a workshop, there is an array of possibilities you could be signing up for, as many workshops consist of a mixture of methodologies while others use just one. Each method is like a different approach to the path, or gateway, through which you can enter into Tantra. You may be drawn into the theory and principles or more to the experience.

At first you may feel a calling very strongly to one or two approaches, but ultimately you are likely to reach a point where it becomes essential to enter all of them, in order to integrate the full spectrum of Tantra. Some people start with the academic study and eventually want to taste the full experience, and so seek practices and experiences. Others delve into experiential Tantra, but after some time wonder what it is all for and where it is leading them, and the theory can help them to place their experiences into a wider context.

To help you choose the right approach of Tantra for you, here follows a summary of the six overriding methods:

1. History, texts and theory

This is when you hear a lecture or talk about an aspect of Tantra, perhaps of its principles, or a verbal teaching of a method that you can later try at home for yourself. Theory alone is not enough to really activate Tantra, but it gives a very good grounding and can help you to integrate your experiences.

You may find a whole school of Tantra that focuses on the history, texts and theory rather than its practices, and some people prefer to do their own study and reading before trying a class or practice.

Studying theory is a safe way to taste Tantra but it is one thing to become an expert on all of the different varieties of fruit in a region, to know all the names in Latin and chemical compounds, but you will not truly know the fruits until you have sunk your teeth into them and allowed the juice to flow into your taste buds. And so it is with Tantric theory.

2. Healing processes

Healing is a large part of Tantra. The root of the word 'healing' comes from 'wholeness' – to become whole. As described in the introduction, Tantra is the weaving together of opposites into wholeness so by its very essence it is a path of healing. Thus any method of Tantra will tend to facilitate healing.

There are also specific healing processes that may be used in workshops, perhaps psychodrama, group therapy, cathartic practices, energy healing or other methods. Often these practices aim to move the participants from shame, guilt and judgement to ease and acceptance of, for example, sexuality, sensuality, nudity, vulnerability or expressing emotions.

Tantra also often addresses the healing between men and women. Age-old wounds from the ubiquitous battle of the sexes can be addressed and healed by those willing to face the ancient pains. This is essential, as the separation between the genders must be brought into unity, in order to experience the transcendence and higher truth of Tantra.

Sexual healing and trauma can also be healed by Tantra. More frequently this is covered in one-on-one sessions rather than group work, so that the student gets more attention in a safer space. This is a sensitive area to address and so it's vital to find a reputable and trustworthy practitioner. Sadly, practitioners are unregulated and so occasionally, it has been the case that a practitioner has re-traumatized their client. As Tantra gains awareness, there are more and more organizations stepping up to create safe and regulated systems of sexual trauma healing (*see Resources, page 241*).

3. Practices

The ancient lineages of Tantra, Tantric yoga and Taoism contain many energy practices and often involve working with the potent sexual energy and learning to channel it through the body.

The most essential practice found throughout Tantra is to 'raise energy', also known as 'sublimation'. Here the strong, heavy, sexual energy is channelled upwards (usually through the spinal column) to the head and crown, thus creating higher states of consciousness and bliss. This practice ranges from very still meditations to full-body orgasmic experiences.

The phrase 'multi-orgasmic practices' tends to conjure up images of classes full of naked people in fully orgasmic states. Whilst classes like that probably do exist somewhere, Tantric practices more commonly look like a yoga or meditation class.

Sometimes practices are done with un-aroused energy (subtle energy), and other times more energy is activated through movement, breathwork or sound. Very few Tantra classes use genital stimulation, yet people can experience becoming quite orgasmic from shaking or breathing in a certain way. We are so used in our society to orgasm being limited to genital orgasm, that it may be hard to grasp how orgasmic we can feel from fully clothed, solo, non-genital practices. Tantra wants to activate this energy, as it is the fuel for healing, transformation and higher states of consciousness.

4. Experiential Tantra

Often in Tantra workshops you will be led through a simulated life situation. Within the held space of the workshop, participants go through experiences with a heightened awareness of them. For example, the facilitator may guide you to dance with people, or to watch someone dance. They may invite you to touch or to look into another person's eyes.

Each experience gives you an opportunity to explore what arises within you. In this held space, you get to play with actions you might not otherwise explore. It is up to the facilitator to hold the space and guide the interactions in ways in which everyone feels safe to open up. This type of Tantra is sometimes thought of as a 'laboratory of life': a chance to explore life and intimacy, whilst being held and guided.

5. Massage

Massage is a powerful medium for the transmission of Tantra. Being completely hands-on, a more experienced Tantric practitioner can actually pass on what is known as 'energy activation' through their touch. Rather than simply aiming to relax the recipient, Tantric massage often activates energies, as well as relaxing the body. This meeting of relaxation and stimulation is one of the core principles of Tantra.

Massage is a great way to teach the principles of Tantra without lovemaking, as an experienced Tantric masseuse can facilitate channelling sexual energy throughout the body. The recipient can thus open up energy channels and have an embodied experience of Tantric energy flow. This will then stay activated and carry over into the recipient's life and relationship.

Tantra is a path that deeply honours the feminine. The types of sexual connection that have become popularized through pornography and modern trends often don't give the time, attention and touch that the female body needs in order to open up. Men can also access more of the sensual and erotic nature through Tantra massage, as well as learning how to prevent or delay ejaculation.

6. Ritual

A very special method used in Tantra is that of ritual. To create a ritual is to create sacred space in which an experience can happen – we'll look at how to create that space in Chapter 5 (*see page 52*) – and couples often use Tantric rituals to increase their intimacy from being just a pleasurable one to a vehicle for sacred experience or altered state of consciousness. A ritual brings a sense of something out of the ordinary and a deeper sense of meaningfulness to experience.

SUMMARY

❖ Finding the right teacher can be a combination of setting a clear intention and then listening to the synchronicities that arise.

❖ Not all who claim to teach Tantra are actually teaching this ancient path, for example those teaching conscious sexuality. There is nothing wrong with conscious sexuality, but it is simply not Tantra.

❖ Beware of the shadow side of Tantra: some teachers may be tempted to misuse their power and take advantage of naïve or vulnerable students.

❖ If you feel you need a safer space, then find a school that has strong and clear boundaries. This is not a concern for all students, but simply know your own choice and follow it.

❖ Tantra can be taught in several different ways, including Tantric theory, healing processes, practices, experiential Tantra, massage and rituals.

Chapter 4

Developing a Tantric Daily Practice

'The way of the superior lover is about practising being who you truly are.'

DAVID DEIDA

Becoming an expert in any area of life takes practice. To become a violinist takes hours and hours, years and years of dedicated practice. To become a world champion skier takes years of being out on the slopes to fine-tune each micro-movement into your body. A Tantra Master is no different. If you wish to play the music of love through your body as an instrument, then you will need to dedicate some time to learning to play the scales.

What are Tantric practices?

A practice, known in Sanskrit as a *sadhana*, is about making a time each day for connecting to the Divine or your true nature. In Tantra, the practices are also used to awaken the life-force energy, which gives the feeling of being more alive and full of vitality. This energy supports our creative process each day and helps us embody our true nature.

Many practices are solo while others can be done with a partner but it's recommended that you do some practices alone, to connect with yourself, before connecting with others.

There are many benefits to incorporating a daily practice into your life, as it allows you to:

❖ Tune in to your highest potential every day, reminding yourself of your direction. Ultimately this is tuning in to the Divine or to your true self.

❖ Open up and allow energy to flow more freely through your body.

❖ Replace old habits of behaviour with a new way of being, one that is aligned with your true self.

❖ Purify emotions so that you release disturbing emotions and live more from love.

❖ Increase your orgasmic potential.

As described in the previous chapter, a Tantric practice may be purely meditation, breathwork, yoga or involve working with energy. It could also be a combination of all of the above or any practice that shifts you from an ordinary state of existence into an altered state. A practice may also be eye-gazing with a partner, sharing breath, moving energy or making love together.

It's best to do your practice first thing in the morning as that way it will set you up for the whole day. You might even like to think of this daily practice as a way to tune in and choose the highest vibration possible, and it is one of the most powerful ways to create your own reality and live the most joyful life.

Your Tantric practice might include breathwork, yoga, qigong or dance and movement so let's look at each one in turn.

Tantric breathwork

There are two main ways of working with the breath in Tantra:

1. *Pranayama*: Deep, slow meditative breathing is often part of yoga practice. It is usually meditative and brings the practitioner into a deep state of peace and inner balance.

2. **Breathwork:** This may be strong breathing that moves a lot of energy. One type is circular breathing, with no pause between inhalations and exhalations. Another is cathartic breathwork, using fast, deep breathing to move blockages and open up. Breathwork can be cathartic, but it can also be experienced as very orgasmic.

Breath and energy have long been closely related in Eastern traditions and medicine. In yogic terminology, the word *prana* means 'energy' but can also be used to mean 'breath' (hence the name, *pranayama*). In Taoist theory the *chi* (energy) and the breath are very closely related, and indeed the breath can be used to carry chi around the body.

Therefore, to move energy, you need to be aware of your breath and it needs to be deep and full and flowing. Think about the breath during orgasm, for example, and how it changes from how you usually breathe. It can become heavy (think of heavy breathing conversations!), faster, full of sighing sounds and so on. Therefore by working on our breath, we can start to awaken and move our sexual energy.

The more aware you become of your breath, the more conscious of your sexual energy and orgasm you become.

In fact the first four sutras of the Tantric text *Vigyan Bhairav Tantra* focus exclusively on the breath. In this text, Shakti asks her beloved Shiva, 'What is the nature of the universe?' She wants to know what is the mystery of all of Existence. Shiva does not give her a direct answer, but instead offers her 112 methods by which she can awaken herself and know the higher truth.

The sutras gave Shakti the guidance she needed and can help us to develop a Tantric breath meditation. You too can try these out. The sutras on the following pages are taken from Paul Reps' version of the *Vigyan Bhairav Tantra*. Set up your sacred space as described in Chapter 5 (*see page 52*) and then simply try one practice at a time. If a particular practice brings you strong results (shifts your state of consciousness, brings you into deep peace, gives you a realization, etc.), then you may want to continue with it for a few days in a row. Alternatively you can move to the next practice.

You can design your practice schedule around the times that suit you best. Usually one practice per meditation sitting is enough, as most people tend to get more from one simple method and entering it deeply than from trying too many different techniques at once.

Practice: Tantric breath meditations

For each of the following meditations set yourself a reasonable time that you can keep up on a daily basis, perhaps 5–10 minutes. Once the practice starts to yield powerful results you may find that you want to extend your time. Some meditators like to practise for 30–60 minutes a day, but generally it is better to do a short practice daily than a longer practice irregularly.

Tantric breath meditation 1

> *'Radiant one, this experience may dawn between
> two breaths. After breath comes in and just
> before turning up – the beneficence.'*

Shiva is telling Shakti that the experience of awakening she seeks can occur in the space between in the in-breath and the out-breath. If she pays attention to that gap, then she may discover the beneficence. This word means 'goodness', but is also another word for God.

1. Sit somewhere peaceful and close your eyes.

2. Begin to watch your breath flowing in and out.

3. Then bring your awareness to the space in between each breath.

In this meditation, you do not need to hold your breath or alter it, simply become aware of the gap.

Tantric breath meditation 2

> *'As breath turns from down to up, and again as breath curves
> from up to down – through both these turns, realize.'*

This meditation is similar to the previous one, but rather than pointing Shakti to the gaps, Shiva is pointing her to the curves. There is a momentum between each breath: the in-breath feels like it goes up and up and up, then it reaches a peak and feels as if it turns. It curves around from this upward direction into a downward direction, and then becomes the out-breath. The out-breath falls and fall and falls, until it turns and becomes again the in-breath rising up.

1. Sit somewhere peaceful and close your eyes.

2. Begin to watch your breath flowing in and out.

3. Now bring awareness to the uprising feeling of the in-breath and the down-falling feeling of the out-breath. Watch the breath rise and fall for a few rounds.

4. Now bring awareness to the change in direction. At what point does it go from upwards to downwards? Just simply watch and observe this turning as fully as you can, as if nothing else exists.

Again, you do not need to hold your breath or alter it, simply become aware of the gap.

Tantric breath meditation 3

> 'Or, whenever in-breath and out-breath fuse, at this instant touch the energy-less, energy-filled centre.'

This is close to the last meditation, but rather than watching the change in direction, you're trying to see how the in-breath and the out-breath actually meet. How do the two breaths fuse together? In what way are they joined?

What is this energy-less, energy-filled centre that Shiva is talking about? This is a paradox and points to a transcendental truth: there is no way to understand paradox through the mind, we must use the meditation to grasp this truth.

1. Sit somewhere peaceful and close your eyes.

2. Begin to watch your breath flowing in and out.

3. Now watch as the in-breath nears it completion, and the same with the out-breath. How does one become the other?

4. Watch very carefully, without holding your breath, as one breath becomes the other. Keep watching the fusion point, the meeting point.

Tantric breath meditation 4

> *'Or when breath is all out and stopped of itself, or all*
> *in and stopped – in such universal pause, one's small*
> *self vanishes. This is difficult only for the impure.'*

This sutra guides Shakti into experimenting with holding the breath. If she exhales the entire breath and then stops the breath, or if she inhales the breath in and then holds... either way, Shiva promises her that 'one's small self vanishes'. This is one of the main spiritual goals of Tantra: to lose the egoic self and remember our true nature: no longer to identify as being a small self, but to merge with the entire universe and experience a oneness with all that is.

This, Shiva says, can be attained by holding the breath, but only if there is a certain purity. It is difficult for the impure. This suggests that this breath-retention meditation is more advanced and will only work once we have attained a certain state of purity.

What does this mean? It is simply guidance to begin with the earlier breath practices (see above) and to practise them daily until you feel that you can shift into an altered state of consciousness with them: you may notice a deep state of peace, or a quietening of the mind. Once this shift happens, you can progress on to the following practice, but if you feel dizzy or light-headed then go back to the first three breath meditations and continue a few weeks longer.

1. Sit somewhere peaceful and close your eyes.

2. Begin to watch your breath flowing in and out.

3. After a while, inhale and hold your breath. However, make sure there is no tension or pressure. You don't want to be anything less than completely relaxed. If this is hard for you, then drop this practice and come back to it at a later time.

4. If the held breath is easy, then hold it for a few seconds and stay aware. Observe your inner world: the energy within you and your awareness. It can help to look up and inwards towards the third-eye region (the point between, and slightly above, your eyebrows). Looking inwardly to the third eye is known to shift our state of consciousness and is often used in meditation.

5. You can try it also with the out-breath.

Breathing meditation should be calm throughout, not like taking a big gulp of air and diving underwater so if, at any point, you feel pressure, immediately release the breath.

Tantra 101

You can find the Tantric breath meditations and many more guided practices online at: ShashiSolluna.com/Tantric-Tools

---

Dynamic breathwork

This is a dynamic practice used to move stagnant energy and blocked emotions. There is no evidence of this being used in classical Tantra, but it is increasingly popular in Neo-Tantra (*see page 19*). There are several types of breathwork that are common, including:

❖ Transformational Breathwork™

❖ Rebirthing™

❖ Quantum Light Breath™

There are also meditations such as Osho's Chakra Breathing™ and Osho's Dynamic Meditation™. The closest equivalent in Classical Tantra would be the 'breath of fire' or 'bellows breathing', which is used in some yogic practices.

These breath techniques are often strong or fast and continuous, with no pause between the in-breath and the out-breath. This is called 'circular breathing'. After a few minutes of this type of breathing, you usually start to feel emotions arising and moving.

If you continue to breathe in this way, you will feel as if you're going on a journey. At first, unpleasant emotions that have been blocked and repressed start to emerge. You may want to scream or shout or cry whilst you breathe. This is the catharsis and happens spontaneously with this breathwork practice. Often after a period of emotional release, you may feel a flood of joyful or ecstatic emotions. Some people even feel orgasmic, and often experience a deep sense of interconnectedness. Many people describe this as a spiritual experience.

Such breathwork is best under the guidance of an experienced facilitator. This is because the emotional release can be very powerful and a bit scary if you are not used to it. The facilitator will be trained to hold space for such strong emotional releases and will stay calm and present with you as it clears.

Tantric yoga

Yoga is now extremely popular in the West. Many gyms host classes and more and more corporate businesses now offer yoga to their employees so it might sound surprising to discover that yoga has Tantric roots. Some scholars even believe that the true root of yoga lies within the ancient Tantric systems. For example, Master Matsyendra presented hatha yoga, including breathwork and meditation, as a way to raise the kundalini (*see below and also page xv*).

Tantra 101

The famous kundalini energy is a life-force energy and usually depicted as a snake coiled up at the sacrum area. When this potent energy is activated it rises up the spine and can feel very orgasmic and leads into higher states of consciousness. However, it is not like a genital orgasm but more of a full-body orgasm. Those who experience the kundalini rising often describe it as 'making love to the universe'. Some forms of Tantric yoga work with uncoiling and uplifting this kundalini energy.

However, not all yoga can call itself Tantric. So what is the difference?

The major difference between Tantric and non-Tantric yoga is the awareness of energy. Many modern yoga paths focus only on the physical postures and techniques. This can make you very fit and flexible, as well as peaceful and balanced. However, it is not designed to awaken your energy the way that classical Tantric yoga does.

Tantric yoga brings awareness to the energy flows in the body, and uses positions and breath to work with that energy. Particular focus lies on the spine and learning to draw kundalini energy up the spine. This is a powerful experience and a solid Tantric path will offer step-by-step guidance for daily practice to enable the energy to rise without any difficulties and you'll find some exercises later in this chapter to help you get started. Moving too much energy too soon can make you feel dizzy, overwhelmed, confused or even mentally unstable. In the same way that running too much voltage through a thin wire will burn it out, it is better to build strong wires first and then raise the current.

Some Tantric practitioners only practice yoga, and others combine yoga and lovemaking practices.

A Tantric yoga practice can dramatically affect the way we make love and the way energy flows through us during lovemaking.

As you discovered in Chapter 2, historically it was common to do many years of Tantric yoga and meditation before taking on a consort and moving into Tantric lovemaking. In the modern world, however, we are more likely to have the sexual encounters first, and later reach for yoga as we look to deepen our experience.

Sexual vitality qigong

Qigong means energy work and the practice originates from Taoism (*see page 12*) rather than classical Tantra. However, learning to move energy through the body is a very helpful practice and a founding principle in the Taoist Sexual Arts.

There are many types of qigong, but some focus specifically on sexual energy: activating it, building it, raising it, circulating it and storing it. In qigong, the sexual energy is understood to be related to the energy of nature and the earth. To build our vitality, we draw this energy up from the earth. Possibly this is why sick people often go to nature to recover their energy.

The spiritual energy is thought to exist above the head, and so the practitioner raises their sexual energy up towards the crown, in a way very similar to Tantric techniques. However, the Taoist Sexual Arts aim to circulate the energy, drawing sexual energy up and drawing the heavenly energy down. The upward flow is like offering our sexual energy up to the heavens, or to Highest Consciousness. The downward flow is like receiving divine grace or a blessing.

The circulation pathway is called the 'microcosmic orbit' or the 'multi-orgasmic channel'. It derives the latter nickname from the fact that when orgasmic energy spins in this cycle, it can go on and on and on in a multi-orgasmic way. We can be in a state of orgasm for a long time with no release or loss of energy.

These practices, like yoga, are also closely related to the breath. Movement, breath, awareness and energy are foundations of the practice in both systems.

Dance and movement

Dance has traditionally been a part of Tantric practice, at least for women, with the *Devadasis* being women who danced in Tantric temples. They used the art form of dance to learn how to move energy through the body in divine frequencies. All forms of dance can enable you to move energy, and modern Tantra workshops often have a lot of dance in them. Freestyle dancing, such as ecstatic dance, is also often found in modern-day Tantra, for both men and women.

Shaking is a particular movement practice found in some lineages of Tantra and is a way to active the kundalini energy described earlier (*see page 40*). The practitioner simply stands and shakes their whole body, often to upbeat music. After about 10 minutes there is often the feeling of no longer trying to shake, but of being shaken. This is a sign that the life-force energy is awakening. It is a very potent practice and can help you become more orgasmic and more likely to experience full-body orgasm.

Energy practices

Breath and yoga both affect the energy but most people will need to start with breathwork and movement to start to feel the energy. However, after some time the practitioner can become so attuned to subtle energy that they can work with their energy without even moving the body or altering their breath.

Another advanced Tantric practice is to enter a state of pure spontaneity, guided by energy rather than by mind or will. When the practitioner allows their body to be moved by the universal force, there is a movement within a state of deep surrender. It can look like tai chi without any form, or like the body has become a piece of seaweed moving in the ocean.

Such spontaneous movement is called the '*Tandava*', which literally means 'the dance of Shiva'. Why is this the dance of God? Because one has surrendered personal will to the will of the Divine. Rather than planning or controlling your movements, you allow them to happen. This movement is also found in Indonesian culture as *latihan* and in Taoist practices as *wu wei* qigong, meaning 'the formless form'.

At this point the practitioner has deeply united their consciousness (Shiva) with their energy (Shakti), a fusion known as 'Divine Union', which leads to deep states of meditation and transcendence.

Tantra 101

Daniel Odier was a seeker who travelled India looking for a Tantric master. After several disappointing attempts, he gave up and decided simply to move into a mountain village and live a simple life. A few months later, he heard of a wild and dangerous Tantrika living in the jungle near his village.

Needless to say, he sought her out. You can read the rest of the story if you choose in *Tantric Quest* by Daniel Odier.

From this woman, Lalita Devi, Daniel received a transmission of the practice of Tandava. He also learned to apply it to a massage technique, in which the spontaneous movement is shared through touch. Daniel returned to the West and has been teaching this technique for many years.

Practice: Tandava

This practice is both incredibly simple and very advanced! Why is that? We have a habit of holding on and controlling everything in our life, which actually makes everything more complicated and also prevents us from surrendering easily. Tandava is to practise returning to simplicity and truth in our full embodiment.

If you feel you are holding on to a lot, you may find it helpful to shake your body or dance wildly for a few moments before you try the Tandava. You can practise this outside in nature, with all of the sounds and forces of nature moving you. Or if you are indoors you may want to play some music without any fixed rhythm. Classical music can work well, or there is plenty of 'new age' music that will work.

The following exercise is based upon Osho's guidance for how to enter the latihan, and you should allow 20–40 minutes for this practice. It is up to you how often you try this. You may want to do it once in a while. If you want to enter it deeply then try every day for 21 days continuously.

1. Stand with your feet grounded on the earth and raise your hands up to the sky. Take a few deep belly breaths.

2. Wait for a few moments until you feel your hands and arms starting to fill up with a presence. Sometimes it feels as if light is falling from the sky and entering you.

3. Once this presence is filling you, you can let it move your body. Your hands and arms may begin to move through space.

4. Movements should be slow, as if you are moving through thick honey. You may feel like a piece of seaweed in the ocean or an astronaut floating in space.

5. Keep your jaw relaxed. You can even hang your mouth open. A tight jaw keeps us in control; a relaxed jaw helps us to surrender.

6. Eyes can be opened or closed as you like, but don't focus on any particular object.

7. Watch your body. You become a passive observer watching each movement unfold. There is no planning or controlling. If you find your mind wanting to jump in and plan a move, choose to surrender it to the Unknown.

8. Your body may stay standing as it unwinds, or it may move towards the floor in sitting or even lying. However, it is in a state of perpetual motion.

9. When you finish, you may want to sit in silent meditation and just be aware.

Tandava for couples

This same movement can also be performed with your beloved. You start in your own spaces near each other and allow yourselves to drop in to the Tandava (as described above). At some point you may find your bodies touch each other, and then you allow the contact to become part of the dance. Watch out for your mind coming in and trying to control touching your partner, and instead try to surrender to just letting the universe bring you in contact.

Wearing a blindfold can make this practice easier, as this prevents the mind from seeing and planning the movements towards your partner. Instead you are unfolding in empty space and if and when the contact happens, you surrender into it, allowing the contact simply to be another force of the universe that moves you.

The core principles of Tantra

As described, Tantra is based upon an understanding that the universe embraces both duality and oneness, honouring individuality yet acknowledging a unifying principle. Before starting your daily practice and stepping onto the path of Tantra, it is helpful to know some of the core principles because these are like the goalposts, or higher vision. Ultimately where the path of Tantra is leading to; and what kind of reality we are creating with our Tantric practice.

We'll explore each of the five core principles of Tantra in more detail in Part II, but they are as follows:

1. **Everything is sacred**: The path of Tantra is about being able to see that. Tantrics act in a way that makes space for sacredness.

2. **Desire can be a path to the Divine**: By meeting desire with full loving awareness, we can return to the state of our original innocence.

3. **Use polarity to attain unity**: Tantrics work with the attraction between apparent opposites, in presence of love to create unity.

4. **Sublimate sexual energy**: A core practice is to learn to raise sexual energy up through the whole body, from sex to superconsciousness.

5. **Transfiguration**: This is the ultimate aim in Tantra: to see the Divine in and through everything.

SUMMARY

- ❖ Developing a daily practice is a good way to activate Tantric energies in the body (Shakti) and to deepen one's presence (Shiva).

- ❖ Practice often starts with the breath. Bringing awareness to the breath is the foundation of many types of meditation, yoga and qigong.

- ❖ Breath can be moved meditatively or more cathartically for different results.

- ❖ Tantric yoga and sexual vitality qigong are both forms of physical exercise that help to awaken and move sexual energy through the body. Though they are physical they have effects on the energy level.

- ❖ Dance and movement may also be taken on as a Tantric practice.

- ❖ *Tandava* is a very special form of practice passed on from ancient Tantric lineages and can teach you how to enter states of bliss.

- ❖ *The core principles of Tantra form the foundations of the path into Tantra and your daily practice.*

Part II

THE CORE PRINCIPLES OF TANTRA

'Tantra acceptance is total;
it doesn't split you.'

Osho

Chapter 5

Principle 1: Everything is Sacred

*'Everywhere is the centre of the
world. Everything is sacred.'*

Black Elk

Tantra operates on the basic understanding that everything is divine. However, we are here in a state of forgetfulness, as if in a play in which we have forgotten our true nature and mistaken ourselves for the roles we play. Those roles, those mistaken identities, make us appear separate from one another, which in turn creates isolation, loneliness, competition, judgement, hatred... the list goes on and on.

But Tantra reminds us that none of this is true: we are one in a state of forgetfulness. Truly we are all aspects of the Divine. Like the rays of the sun, the rays are actually inseparable from that sun. However, it is easy to become so used to our own unique ray-ness and act as if they were not part of that one same sun, and this is the root cause of suffering.

*To honour everything as sacred, is to treat everything
like a ray of that one divine sun. Through loving
one another we can remember who we are.*

Creating sacredness in everyday life

We can turn any everyday ordinary event into a ritual. The traditional Taoist tea ceremony is a great example of this, in which the ordinary act of drinking tea is treated as a sacred act. We can also turn any space into a temple, seeing it beyond its mere utilitarian purpose and allowing it to become a sacred space.

In Tantra, the bedroom is frequently turned into a temple of love. The intimate relationship is frequently treated as a divine meeting. Of course there are still times in a relationship when you need to be practical and get the food on the table or the kids to school. But as well as this, time and space need to be made for honouring the sacred.

Sacred time

Commit a period of time to be your sacred time on a regular basis. For example, you might choose 20 minutes a day to sit in meditation plus two hours every week for extended practice (either alone or with your partner). Creating time that is committed to sacred experience is a powerful way to bring more divinity, depth and meaning into your life.

A love temple

Choose a physical space to be your love temple, either by having a dedicated area in your house to always be the temple, or creating it before each practice. Some people do a fusion of the two, perhaps with a permanent altar in a room, and lighting candles and/or burning incense before rituals to bring the temple to life.

You can be as creative as you like, using colours, fabrics, images, crystals and/or statues that imbue a sense of sacred for you. Remember that this means anything that lifts you out of the ordinary; an altar can be as simple as a single candle on a table or mantelpiece.

If you want to give your sacred space a Tantric flavour, you could add an appropriate image or statue. For example, the *yab-yum* in which Shiva and Shakti, the God and Goddess are sitting in an embrace. The yab-yum is a lovemaking position in which the woman sits in the lap of the man. Both are sitting up, whilst in union. Thus, it is a combination of lovemaking and meditation.

The yab-yum, a classic image used especially in Tibetan Tantra.

Other Tantric symbols are snakes intertwining, the Shiva-lingam (an Indian statue frequently found in temples which symbolizes the penis in the vagina), Tibetan *tankas* (Tantric paintings) or statues of Tantric gods and goddesses. You may also feel drawn to a specific *yantra* – a geometrical image designed to activate energies (*see page 179*).

There is something very powerful about placing an image or a statue of gods and goddesses in union on your altar: you are placing the sexual act into a divine place; uplifting sexual union from something sordid and shameful and placing it as something profound and sacred.

It is good to do your Tantric practices in your love temple, as well as partner exercises (if you are in a couple). Tantric practices help to generate energy and will charge up your temple space. Meditating in a space helps to bring a sense of presence to that space. After a while, anyone who enters your temple may experience a shift in consciousness, as a result of your practices.

Consecration

To consecrate something is to offer it to the Divine. It is also a way to bring blessings and invite the presence of Grace. Tantrics often consecrate not only their spaces, but they may consecrate the whole act of lovemaking too. Offering your spaces and your actions to the Highest Consciousness is a way of making the choice to act from your true self and not from egoic self.

Practice: Offering to the Divine

You can make a consecration using your own words. Most of all it is about being in a state of devotion and with an open heart.

1. Sit in your love temple and put you hands into prayer position and say, 'I offer this space to Highest Consciousness, and invite Pure Presence into this space. May this space be blessed.'

2. After saying the words (out loud or in your head), sit in silence and feel the space around you. Feel pure Presence filling it.

3. When you feel complete, you can make a small bow to the Mystery. Your space is now blessed.

Even if you struggle with the idea of the Divine, you can still practise Tantra. There is no need to believe in something you have not yet experienced. If it is helpful you can drop the words 'God', 'Divine' or 'Shiva'.

Instead, I invite you to think of a moment in your life when you felt touched by something bigger than you. It might be when you were in some awesome place in nature, standing looking over a great canyon or a stunning view, and for a moment you felt part of a bigger picture – that 'wow' factor, that sense of something bigger than you – that you can call 'Highest Consciousness' or 'Highest Love'. In fact you can call it whatever you like, but this is what you can offer your practices to and seek to connect with through your Tantric experiences.

Other moments might be:

✦ Dancing and letting go of yourself, getting lost in the music, rhythm and your body's expression. When you lose yourself, who is there?

✦ Listening to music or making music that carries you beyond your worldly concerns into a higher space. What is this higher space?

✦ Doing some sport or activity that takes you to your edge: white water rafting, bungee jumping, skydiving, etc. – you get the picture! In the intensity of the moment, you leave yourself behind and get completely absorbed into the moment. What is that moment?

✦ Making love and the energy and passion takes you like a huge ocean wave that carries you upon it. You surrender to that force. What is that force?

These experiences all point you to the Divine! They all point to something conscious that you recognize and are instinctively drawn towards (and at the same time often afraid of!). Something bigger that you, and yet you are a part of it. Knowing God is not necessarily about seeing angels, it is about finding yourself beyond the limitations of your personality.

Creating sacred space together

Once you have sacred time and a sacred temple, the final ingredient is to bring your practice. If you are alone, you can sit and do solo practices in the love temple. You may also choose to do some of the partner practices with a mirror in front of you.

Tantra 101

Once the temple is prepared with music, candles and incense, you may also want to invite your partner into the space. You can sit together opposite one another. A typical opening is to bow to one another with hands in prayer position and say, 'Namaste beloved.' *Namaste* means 'I bow to you'.

. . . .

Practice: Eye-gazing

Eye-gazing yourself is a very powerful practice: self-love is what paves the way to attract more love into our life.

1. Sit in front of a large mirror.

2. Take a deep breath in and a big sigh out.

3. Start to look deep into your own eyes, one eye at a time. Take at least 1 minute with each eye before switching to look in the other.

4. There is nothing to do or to try to make happen, simply gaze into your eyes.

5. Allow about 10 minutes for the whole practice.

If you want to try this practice with your partner:

1. Sit in front of your partner.

2. Take a deep breath in together and a big sigh out at the same time.

3. Start to look deep into your partner's eyes, one eye at a time. Take at least 1 minute with each eye before switching to look in the other.

4. There is nothing to do or to try to make happen, simply gaze into each other's eyes.

5. Allow about 10 minutes for the whole practice.

Overcoming awkwardness

For many people to honour one another in such a way feels silly and stupid, especially if you have been relating together for some time and have never done anything like this before. We are generally somewhat awkward about acknowledging our divine nature. In Asian cultures it is perfectly normal to place hands in a prayer position and bow to one another, but in the West we are more likely to shake hands when we meet or perhaps give a high five.

In the Tantric world, men and women greet each other as gods and goddesses, but in the everyday Western world people may be casual or even derogatory upon meeting. I remember working one summer in an office in the UK where people would greet each other with phrases like, 'Oh bloody hell, not you again'. It took me a while to figure that this was their way of saying 'good morning'.

With this kind of 'cool' behaviour, it is very difficult to be sincerely sacred. I always say:

'Being too cool is the biggest passion-killer!'

The cool and sarcastic mannerisms of modern life are generally not conducive to living through an open heart. You may have to choose to overcome being cool or sarcastic in order to begin to express something more sacred and honouring.

However, there is no reason for faking things, or pushing yourself too far out of your comfort zone. If something feels fake then there is no point doing it. It also does not have to be too serious. It is better to find the most authentic way to be in each moment. This may be eye-gazing together (see above). If this feels too awkward, then just sit with eyes closed holding hands. After a while you will sink into relaxation in this posture and begin to find your truth within it. If awkwardness arises, just take a deep breath and be present with the feeling of awkwardness!

Take your Tantric experience step by step, and this way you can let it evolve authentically.

SUMMARY

❖   Tantra holds that everything is sacred.

❖   Sacredness is a matter of the presence that we hold as we experience something rather than an inherent quality within the thing itself.

❖   We can make time and space for an experience to make it sacred.

❖   Creating a love temple is a good way to bring Tantra into your everyday life.

❖   Meeting yourself or meeting your beloved in sacred space is a good way to remember that everything is sacred.

❖   You may feel awkward from time to time; a shift is happening. Just be present with the sensations arising. As we move into the sacred it can feel strange at first as we drop comfortable masks, but keep breathing!

Chapter 6

Principle 2: Desire is a Path to the Divine

'By far the highest attainment in Tantra is to remain desireless at the peak of desire.'

<small>MARGOT ANAND, *SEX TO SPIRIT* FILM</small>

Many spiritual paths see desire as the biggest blockage: how can you become present when you have desire arising? Many meditators find that sexual obsession causes distraction from the state of meditation. Thus they might employ methods such as imagining the body as rotting meat in order to try to overcome physical desire. Monks and nuns of most traditions, from Christianity to Buddhism, choose celibacy as a method to overcome physical desire and focus instead on spiritual experience. The genders may be kept separate, and the practitioners avoid sexual arousal by dressing modestly.

Tantra does not see desire as a block, but as a key. Tantra does not say to follow all desire indiscriminately, but nor to block and repress it. Tantra invites the bringing of conscious awareness to desire, and it offers methods of working with the energy that is held within desire. If you can become present with desire itself, then you will develop a potent presence, like the eye of the storm.

It is important to understand that Tantra is not the same as hedonism. Hedonism is the path of pleasure that simply invites one to follow all pleasure and all desire, and get lost in pleasure. In history and mythology, hedonism often peaks just before an empire collapses, a symbol that when you follow desire without awareness it can possess you and ruin you. This indiscriminate satiation of desire is not the aim of Tantra. Rather than becoming fixated on the object of desire, in Tantra we become focused on the feeling of the desire itself, and ultimately we find the source of desire within.

Tantra invites healing and awareness though desire.

A guiding principle in Tantra is that of personal will (ego) versus divine will (soul). When we live in the perception of being separate from other people, and separate from life, we also develop personal desires to serve this illusory separate self (called the 'ego'). These desires serve only the personal self and thus only generate an even bigger sense of separateness, creating more suffering and pain ultimately.

Personal desire is cut off from our true nature. It serves the ego, not the true self. However, if we feel guilty about our desires then they become cut off from the light of our conscious awareness, and thus shadow desires – those we act out secretly or repress. These shadow desires are fraught with guilt and shame. Think of sneaking down into the kitchen to take cake from the fridge at night, or looking at porn under the bedcovers so that no one finds out. Or we may seek the company of others who share that shadow desire as a way to try to alleviate our feelings of guilt and shame – seeking our 'partners in crime'. These are shadow desires. It's not about what we do, but the way in which we do it.

As you begin to bring consciousness to your desire something begins to transform. When desire meets the light of conscious awareness, the guilt and shame start to drop away. The desire itself begins to transform; your desire starts to serve consciousness, rather than serving the illusory self. Instead of creating more separation and pain, your desires start to lead you towards your true path.

This shift can be seen as accessing divine desire and aligning with divine will. This in effect means dropping the ego and becoming our true nature. What this entails is that rather than our actions being to try and fulfil our own personal wants and needs, we start to tune in to our higher self and our higher purpose. Our desires naturally start to serve the bigger picture rather than the personal self. This is not something that we try to do – like acting piously or trying to do the right thing – but happens naturally as we work consciously with desire through Tantra.

This is healing because our desire becomes part of the whole again. Egoic desire often seeks to hurt or harm another for its own pleasure. It is separate from the whole. But divine desire could never harm another; it is in alignment with the interconnected nature of all things.

The ultimate desire is to love.

Until we desire only love – to give, to receive and to be love – then we still have healing to do on our Tantric path.

Divine desire and the collective consciousness

One remarkable feature of shifting from personal desire to divine desire is that when we live out our divine desire, we align with an ultimate truth that is true to all beings. What this means is that if we were all to move from personal desire to divine desire, then we would shift from separation to unity. When everyone is living out his or her divine desire, the collective enters a state of Unity Consciousness, which is pure love.

When we live out our personal desires they often conflict with other people's desires and needs, and there is a sense of competition. We feel we have to fight for limited resources. However, as we shift into living our divine desire, our soul's purpose, we tune in to a higher truth in which there is no separation. If many people make this shift together (as in a Tantric community or in a ritual) then a state of perfect creative unfolding can be attained in which there is no more sense of personal desire taking anything from anyone else.

Collective consciousness

I often teach Tantra groups and festivals where I witness absolute miracles happening. When a whole group of people raise their energy together – shares a united intention of living as love – the personal conflicts start to rise and then fall away... making space for a unified field of creativity to emerge.

Issues arising usually characterize the first few days of a festival or event. We often use the structure of sharing circles, in which people get into small groups and are able to share what's going on for them and be heard by the rest of the group without judgement. This enables old patterns and fears to arise and fall away.

At the same time we use Tantric practices to raise energy and so the whole vibration starts to rise, and an incredible and tangible energy of creativity and spontaneity starts to appear. Everyone is dancing, laughing, hugging, and a unified field is developed in which conflicting interests have dissolved. One person's desire is another's desire. One person's creativity flows effortlessly with another's. We fall into rhythm and harmony together. We dance as one body of love.

Whenever I see this, I know this is our destiny. I always think to myself: if this is possible with 100, with 500, with 1,000 people then it must be possible with more. Is there any limit to the number of people who can enter this unified field? It must be possible for a world to wake up to divine desire and our highest purpose and to live together as love. But hey, I like to think big!

SUMMARY

* Many spiritual paths work by eliminating desire; however, Tantra uses desire as a pathway to realization.

* It is seen as an ideal opportunity for meditation: to learn to stay present in the midst of desire.

* There is also a shift from personal desire to divine desire as we awaken.

* Ultimately if a whole community shifts into divine desire, then a pure creative space is attained in which there is no more sense of competition or separation.

Chapter 7

Principle 3: Use Polarity to Attain Unity

*'Sexual attraction is based on sexual polarity.
All natural forces flow between two poles... The
masculine and feminine poles between people
create a flow of sexual energy in motion.'*

DAVID DEIDA

Many spiritual paths aim to reach immediately into what is known as 'unity consciousness' or 'oneness'. However, Tantra acknowledges this life as a play of opposites or polarities. Tantra is not afraid to play with polarity, and actually uses it as a vehicle to attaining oneness-realization. In other words, Tantra embraces everything from our most human individual experience to the highest level of interconnectedness with all that is. Tantra has a way of embracing dualism and non-dualism.

There is another path, also rooted in Indian philosophy, known as *Vedanta* (a path of oneness or non-duality). This path would call all opposites '*maya*' meaning 'illusion', and tends to dismiss them. Thus emotions and feelings may all be cast aside, and vedantics may choose asceticism (giving up worldly pleasures) in order to know oneness.

Tantra, however, embraces the opposite forces of the universe and *uses* them to know oneness. Tantra works with the alchemy of union, to bring these opposites together in the presence of love in order to create a transcendental experience.

This concept may sound very high and far off, but think of a time you felt a lot of opposition to someone, and then somehow both of your hearts opened and you received each other. For example, you may have held an opposing opinion to someone. But then for some reason you both allowed the other's opinion without fighting it. You met the other person in love and acceptance instead of conflict. Do you remember the rush of love in that moment? Polarity can actually *generate love*. We can make love with polarity, and this is why Tantra embraces it. Not only can we make love but there is also an understanding that we are *here* to awaken through this dance of polarity.

Tantra understands all of reality as a dance between opposites, which it calls 'Shiva' and 'Shakti'. These are the masculine and feminine principles in life, which can be personified and seen as divine lovers (*see page 34*). Please note that these are not gender identities *per se*, but are about two opposing forces in reality. All of us, men and women, contain both forces. We may identify more strongly with one or the other. Or we may play out one or the other in relationship with someone else. But we are not limited to one or other type of polarity.

Each of us is whole and complete as we are,
and yet we can experience ourselves relative to
others. This is part of the divine game of life.

Women tend to feel more resonance with Shakti qualities while men may feel more aligned with Shiva aspects, but this is not the only way and our polarity changes over time and also relative to whom we are with. This is irrespective of gender. However, we usually experience one polarity externally and the Tantric journey of relating is to unleash our inner opposite and thus become whole once more.

Whatever you experience more as your predominant expression, remember that the opposite exists within you. This is like the concept in psychotherapy of having an inner man or inner woman. You may be externally very Shakti, identified with the flow of energy and feelings moment to moment, but within you have a core of Shiva awareness waiting to awaken. Or you may identify with more 'Shiva' qualities of presence and awareness, but within you are deep feelings and energy flows waiting to awaken. We can awaken these by relating with someone who expresses that opposite, and usually we are attracted to that kind of person. Hence the popular adage 'opposites attract'. In Tantra we take that a step farther:

Opposites attract and awaken each other.

Our sexual polarity is an individual experience, shaped by many factors in our lives, including physical disposition, genes and upbringing. Our sexual polarity can also change over time, and change in different relationships. Some people have a strong polarity in one direction, others move between the two from moment to moment. Others do not even experience much polarity and feel neutral much of the time (these people are less likely to be attracted to Tantra). It doesn't matter which you are in any moment, as the Tantric definitions are to help your understanding rather than for judgement. Ultimately we must remember that these polarities are relative terms, not absolute.

> *We are in a world that appears to be made of*
> *opposites, falling in love with those opposites*
> *in order that we can reawaken to our totality.*

Tantric polarity

All of life can be understood as a dance between Shiva and Shakti: a play of consciousness and energy.

❖ **Shiva**, the masculine principle, is the witness, stillness and meditative awareness. It is the part of us that never changes, but sits and watches life. *Shiva* is used to mean consciousness or awareness.

❖ **Shakti**, the feminine principle, is the dance of life. The feelings, emotions and energies that move as life moves. *Shakti* is used to mean energy or power.

For example, when you have a strong emotional experience such as an outburst of anger or an outpouring of grief, you may be more in your Shiva, in which case you witness the emotion in a detached way, as if separate from it. You may be more in your Shakti and feel the emotion fully as a huge surge of energy running through you, and you surrender completely to that flow.

In Tantra the aim is to unite Shiva and Shakti.

What does this mean?

First, it means that if one polarity is sleeping within you, you must awaken it. Second, it means that we need to heal any separation between the two polarities, internally and externally. So if, for example, a man and woman fight a lot in a relationship, this often means that there is an inner battle going on in each individual between their masculine and feminine aspects.

Do some self-reflection using the notes below, to discover if you have an imbalance within yourself. Is your masculine side or your feminine side over-dominant?

Tantra 101

Use the following descriptions to assess whether there is any imbalance between your Shiva and Shakti aspects:

Excess of Shiva: You are too detached from your feelings, you may want to activate more energy and develop your feminine side more. This could be done by dancing for example or by meditating to feel energy flow or by loving a feminine person.

Excess of Shakti: If you are chaotic and confused and get bashed around by your own emotions, then you may want to develop more awareness to hold space for your experiences. Practising mindfulness meditation, for example, or by loving a masculine person, could do this.

Loving a person with qualities that you hope to awaken within yourself is not about stealing that quality from them or taking their energy. It is an awakening of inner qualities because the act of love has an alchemical effect.

For example, if a man suppresses his tears for many years, in the belief that 'men don't cry', when he deeply loves a woman who expresses her tears naturally, he loves even her tears. In that moment, he forgives also his own tears; he forgives his own inner feminine. An inner alchemy occurs as the man softens and his inner feminine awakens to balance his masculine. This is how loving a person with apparently opposite qualities can help us to heal and become whole.

Alternatively a woman may be afraid to be more adventurous and try new activities, such a rock climbing or surfing. When she loves and trusts a man, he can carry her through such challenges that she could not do alone and thus initiate her into them. The strong masculine direction can help her move through fears and resistance and so awaken more Shiva within her.

Uniting Shiva and Shakti

Once you have awakened Shiva and Shakti within, then you will need to unite them. You may have an activated emotional, flowing intuition and have the directional, witnessing aspect, and the next step is to ask: how do these two relate together?

Imagine you have an inner relationship. How does your man hold your woman? How does your masculine create a structure to hold your feminine creativity? How does your inner witness hold space for your feminine flow of emotions? How easily does your feminine flow surrender to your masculine direction? If your inner masculine is a control freak and your inner feminine is in chaos, then ask yourself: how can these two move into a harmonious relationship?

Exercise: Gestalt Therapy for the inner union

This is a version of the Gestalt 'Empty Chair' method. It is a simple but powerful form of aspecting, in which you allow your two inner parts to have a conversation and resolve any conflicts or separation.

1.   Get three cushions and sit on the floor on one of them and place the other two in front of you, facing each other.

2.   Choose one to represent your inner masculine and the other your inner feminine.

3.   Sit in whichever cushion wants to speak first and face the other. Let words come (without thinking about it first!), and use the word 'I' for that aspect. For example: 'I am the inner feminine and I feel...' and then tell the inner masculine how she feels.

4.   Then switch cushions and reply from the opposite aspect.

5.   Keep changing cushions to have a conversation. It can go in any direction, just let each aspect speak and be heard.

6.   After some time, see if there is any kind of resolution that is needed. For example, if one aspect has been ignoring the other, then that aspect could apologize and agree to listen more.

7.   At the end of the exercise bow down to the opposite cushion to say 'Thank you'. Then switch and let the other bow down in gratitude.

This exercise can be surprising and reveal deep unconscious patterns. Do not try to plan the conversation, but rather let it unfold at the time.

You can also do the same exercise but with a friend or your partner sitting silently with you and witnessing your process.

Finding peace through polarity

Once the inner masculine and feminine are more united, then you are able to allow a full flow of emotions and energy (Shakti) whilst being able to stay fully present with them (Shiva). Eventually this leads to a lot more inner peace. Emotions only carry a lot of charge when they feel the need to be heard/seen/witnessed. As we bring consciousness to the energy of the shadow emotions, a healing occurs. Those shadow emotions are brought into the light, and what we once experienced as troubling emotions are resolved.

Two people are usually attracted to one another because of polarities and can use Tantra in their relationship to balance and unite the opposite forces within them. Meditations of energy exchange are good practices for this, as is the 'circle of light' practice given later in this chapter (*see page 80*), as it uses polarity to build energy.

Is polarity politically incorrect?

In this age of equality, the principle of polarity can provoke controversial reactions in people when they first encounter it. But it is best understood as a game or art, rather than as a gender role or identity. If you and I wanted to play chess, one of us would have to be white and the other black in order to play together and generate an exciting game. If we both wanted to be grey, we would have a great sense of equality, but a boring game indeed!

And so it is with polarity. You can explore your own masculine or your own feminine with your partner. You can discover how they interact and play. And ultimately you can bring them together in love, and dissolve beyond all separation into the oneness of our higher nature. You could also choose to play another game altogether... that is up to you!

> *Polarity is not limited, and we are not confined to one half of it. Polarity is relative and changeable, from one relationship or circumstance to another.*

Ways of playing with polarity in partnership

There are unlimited ways for Shiva and Shakti to dance and play, but below are a list of examples. It says Shiva and Shakti, which is irrespective of the actual gender of the person playing.

❖ Shakti dances and Shiva watches.

❖ Shiva guides and Shakti follows (for example in traditional ballroom dancing).

❖ Shakti expresses emotions and feelings and Shiva holds space with deep presence.

❖ Shakti massages whilst Shiva receives and witnesses the experience in the body.

❖ Shakti puts on beautiful radiant clothing and Shiva admires and observes.

Tantra also understands lovemaking as containing a large amount of Shiva–Shakti play. One partner may penetrate whilst the other receives. One partner may be on top giving the direction to the act, whilst the other lies beneath and surrenders to the guidance. A couple may always play the same role, or they may switch.

Not all lovemaking is so polarized and with more subtle lovemaking the couple may simply unite. The famous Tantric yab-yum lovemaking position (*see page 53*) is a balanced position in which the man and woman are both sitting in union, no partner on top. It is often used in the later stages of lovemaking after the polarity energies have played themselves out, and the couple is ready to move into a more meditative and balanced meeting.

> *In Tantra there is no better or worse way, but rather the understanding that our bodies know what we need in each moment.*

Exercise: Shiva–Shakti scale

Where do you currently fall on the Shiva–Shakti scale? Read the following statements and answer YES if you agree overall with each one.

Part 1

❖ I prefer to be alone in silence rather than in the middle of noisy gatherings. I'd rather go fishing, or immerse myself in a project on my computer, or work in my shed in the garden rather than attend a big family get-together.

❖ I like sports and hobbies with the element of danger or risk in them (e.g. surfing, rock-climbing, gambling, etc.).

❖ I like clear spaces with clean lines, minimalist décor.

❖ I prefer a war or action movie over a romance.

❖ I like wearing simple colours, like black or white.

Part 2

❖ I prefer to be in gathering of family or friends, with lots of time for chatting and catching up, rather than to be alone.

❖ I like sports and hobbies that are fun and playful, such as dance, crafts and massage.

❖ I like warm and cosy spaces that seem homely and welcoming.

❖ I prefer a romance movie over a war or action film.

❖ I like to wear bright and colourful clothing with lots of accessories.

Add up the number of yeses. If you have more in Part 1, then you have a strong Shiva polarity. If you have many more in Part 2, you have a strong Shakti polarity. If you have equal yeses or found it hard to agree with any of the statements, then you may be less polarized and more balanced within yourself.

Those who are more strongly polarized tend to be much more drawn to relating and sexuality, whereas those who are balanced within themselves may be just as happy on their own. There is no better or worse in Tantra. We simply use this information to understand ourselves, and where we are at, and throw some light upon our relationships and attractions.

In general, strongly polarized people will be attracted to one another. So someone with a lot of Shiva characteristics will be attracted to someone with a lot of Shakti characteristics. Those with more balance may be drawn to others who are balanced.

Polarity generates energy

Tantrics may choose to play with or enhance polarity between couples because a strong polarity generates a strong charge. Just as a battery needs a positive and a negative to create power, so we can play with polarity, and the bigger the differential between the poles, the stronger the charge. Thus a couple (of any gender) can play with polarity to generate charge and attraction.

A simple example of this is when the feminine partner chooses to dance (dancing moves energy and is a Shakti activity) and the masculine partner may choose to watch (witnessing is more meditative and a Shiva quality). When the feminine partner is watched, they often feel a lot more energy move than when they dance alone. When the masculine partner has a dancer to witness, he may become more present than if he were staring into empty space. This is a situation in which energy and awareness are interacting.

Often the attraction and charge between couples becomes even stronger when they play with polarity in such a way. After the polarized activity, they may want to unite together and make love. At this point, the opposing forces are drawn together and merge, taking both participants into a state of oneness. If the couple practise Tantric lovemaking, they will consciously channel these energies higher to facilitate a transcendental experience.

Thus polarity is used to create an experience of returning to Unity, and this is the dance of Tantra, known as 'divine union'.

Exercise: Playing with polarity

Think about an experience you've had in which you were playing one polarity with someone playing the opposite. Maybe you were dancing and being watched; or you were watching a dance. Maybe you had a night with your friends and then later reunited with your partner.

❖ How did you feel within your own polarity?

❖ How did you feel in relation to the other? Were you afraid of being seen or of meeting the opposite? Were you excited? Was there energy aroused by this?

Tantra 101

When playing with polarity it is wise always to keep unity as your highest goal. If you do not, then you run the risk of creating more separation rather than creating love. The highest goal is to generate love. So if you strongly identify with your role and see only your differences from your partner, then you may end up making separation and conflict.

Polarity is a game: it looks as if we are separate and different, but actually we are all total in and of ourselves. Our beloved is simply awakening what is inside us. If you are attracted to masculine lovers, then let them awaken the masculine within you. If you are attracted to those with feminine qualities, allow your own inner feminine to flower in their presence. We are here to remember our totality and oneness. By loving what we once thought was opposite and different, we are uniting opposites, and awakening all within ourselves.

Practice: Circle of light

This practice can help couples exchange masculine and feminine energies. If you are in a same-sex couple, then simply decide who wants to be in each role. The circle of light is based on the polarity of the body. The effects of this practice are that you can work with the attraction of opposites to generate energy. That energy then circles between you and your partner's bodies, having the effect of balancing yin and yang in both of you. It can give you the feeling of opening up, coming together in deeper intimacy and also can bring you into a state of Higher Consciousness.

In a man's body the sex centre is yang, or a positive pole: it penetrates into the world. In a woman's body, the sex centre goes inwards and thus is a yin or receptive pole. Like two batteries, there is a + and a − pole that are attracted. (In same-sex couples there may be one who is the penetrator and one the receiver. For the purposes of this exercise just choose who is in each position).

The other centre in this meditation is the heart centre. In a woman's body this is yang as we can see from her breasts that her love penetrates the world. A man's heart is relatively receptive, and thus is his yin pole.

So to activate the circle of light, you and your partner breathe together, each exhaling out of the positive pole and inhaling into the receptive pole. At first this exercise can be a little confusing with the inhale/exhale and hand movements, but once you have it going it is easy.

1. Sit together facing each other with your knees close enough to touch. Hold each other's hands, rested on your knees for comfort.

2. Start with a few moments of eyes closed, deepening the breath to connect with yourself.

3. Once you are ready to connect, squeeze your hands as a signal and you can both open your eyes and take a few moments to eye-gaze and breathe together.

4. The woman (or the sexually receptive partner) will initiate the movements and pace of the exercise. She starts by inhaling and drawing both hands towards her sexual centre, as if taking in his sexual energy, and then upwards to her heart area.

5. As she exhales she pushes the hands forwards from her heart to his, as if giving love energy to him.

6. The man then mirrors the breath: as she inhales, he exhales. So as she takes sexual energy into her sex centre with an in-breath, he offers sexual energy out of his sex centre with an out-breath. As she exhales love from her heart, he inhales love into his heart, and then all the way down to his sex centre.

7. Continue to breathe and follow the flow of energy: this is the circle of energy, the circle of light. Sometimes it speeds up and other times it becomes slow and subtle.

8. After 10 minutes of energy flow, rest your hands and lean forwards with your foreheads gently resting together. Rest for 3 minutes in this position with eyes closed, to enter meditation with the energy.

9. Complete with a bow to each other and a hug. Some couples like to move into lovemaking after this meditation.

For a guided download of this practice go to: ShashiSolluna.com/Tantric-Tools

Inner Union: Uniting the polarity within with meditation

One of the highest meditation practices in Tantra is known as 'inner union', and all outer union actually points us back to this. Inner union is when our own apparently opposite qualities or aspects unite and merge. This inner union is a large part of the right-handed path of Tantra, in which a Tantric practitioner abstains from intercourse. However, even for someone who is sexually active or in a relationship, it is helpful to look within to see one's own inner polarity.

These meditations are a great way to follow up the Gestalt exercise (*see page 73*).

Many of the solo Tantric practices are working with different forms of uniting consciousness and energy. For example:

❖ Consciousness (Shiva) watches the breath (Shakti).

❖ Consciousness (Shiva) watches inner flows of energy (Shakti).

❖ Consciousness (Shiva) watches the senses (Shakti).

❖ Consciousness (Shiva) observes emotions (Shakti).

❖ Consciousness (Shiva) observes orgasm and sexual energy flows (Shakti).

The result of turning life events into meditations is that a profound inner union can occur. It is not about Shiva controlling Shakti; it's not about Consciousness controlling energy/emotions/senses. It is really about practising until one reaches the recognition that they are truly one. This is the knowing that all emotion is the manifestation of consciousness. And thus that all of life is the manifestation of God.

This cannot truly be grasped by reading about it. There is no alternative but to sit and become immersed into a practice, and simply allow the union and awakening to reveal itself. Most of the practices in this book can facilitate this process.

Divine union

I was attending a 10-day silent retreat at a Tantra school called Agama Yoga, practising meditations of Kashmiri Shaivism and moving between devotion and meditation alternately. In devotional practices we would get into an ecstatic bliss by chanting or praying. These practices are called 'Shaktopaya' because they are working with Shakti energy. This blissful energetic state is called 'bhavana' meaning 'to be filled with bhav *is to be filled with bliss'.*

Then we would switch to total meditation practices. Focusing on the sound within: 'I am', or an inner mantra in Sanskrit and so falling into deep recognition of our true nature as the eternal presence of Shiva. This style of practice is called Shivopaya *because it focuses on our Shiva nature.*

And we would move from Shaktopaya to Shivopaya to Shaktopaya to Shivopaya. From 'I worship God' to 'I am God' to 'I worship God' to 'I am God'.

Now until this moment, I hadn't realized how I still carried an inner split between these two states. In the past I had done plenty of Shaktopaya, in the form of devotional singing and prayer, and plenty of Shivopaya, in the form of meditation and self-realization practices, including a lot of Buddhist practices, but without realizing that these two were heavily polarized within me. They were split. I would either practise one or the other, but never did the two forms meet.

In fact there was a subtle war within me, because at Buddhist retreats I denied my devotional side, and dismissed those practices. But put me in a room full of Hare Krishnas and I would quickly enter full devotional chanting and ecstasy and deny all of my Buddhist practices in an instant of ecstasy!

Yet here I was, in a Tantric retreat switching from one to the other and building all of the energy above the crown of my head (the energetic focus of these practices).

It felt like a nuclear explosion was building at my crown. My devotional ecstatic energy rising, yet my meditational focused energy accumulating. The two felt like they were going to fight each other... and then suddenly... boom! An energetic nuclear explosion happened right above my crown. The two united in one glorious moment and all separation was instantly transcended.

It was like being transported instantly into the Divine. Everything was golden. I could see the goodness inherent in all things: the goodness of the nature of existence. I was filled with a feeling that I can only call 'Hallelujah'. I was in the bliss of being. I rested there because there was nowhere else to go! The beauty of the truth that revealed itself was so glorious that no other state of reality could possibly call me away. I wept in joy at the beauty of the Truth.

That moment changed my life because, while the blissful hallelujah state only lasted a few days, I had seen that no separation is as real as it appears, and when we can open our minds wide enough to allow the paradox to exist... then the truth can be revealed. And the truth is love. The truth is golden.

SUMMARY

❖ Polarity is a part of nature: this world is made up of dark and light, of warm and cold, of masculine and feminine.

❖ You can find out whether you have a stronger masculine or feminine, but also see how the opposite polarity plays out within you. If there is a conflict within you, it is likely to play out as a conflict in your external relationships.

❖ There is a magical force between polar opposites, a force of attraction. Energy runs between them and this energy can activate and awaken us if we choose to use it.

❖ Understanding polarity can help us understand the sexual force and sexual attraction.

❖ When we can bring two polarities together in totality, then we can enter the transcendent state, or Source. It is very blissful to attain this state.

Chapter 8
Principle 4: Sublimate Sexual Energy

'This is the Tantric definition of our sexuality: the return to absolute innocence, absolute oneness.'

Osho

Whether you practise sexual or non-sexual Tantra a core feature of both paths is to 'sublimate' sexual energy. In other words, learn to raise sexual energy up through your body to raise consciousness and induce a state of bliss. Some people even enter a state known as *satori*, meaning 'realization', in which they have an awakening experience.

In 'normal' non-Tantric sex, the sexual energy is often built up under tension until the body cannot contain it any more and it is released out of the body as an ejaculation (in men) or a tension-release orgasm (in men and women). You can compare it to filling up a balloon with water. You fill it up and the balloon gets tighter and tighter until it cannot contain the water any more and it bursts, releasing the water all over the floor. Afterwards there is a sense of relief.

For many people sex has become about this sense of release of tension and the relief it brings. Partners may even start to use one another just to release their pent-up tensions and some get addicted to this kind of sex, just because of the release. A common situation that arises from such sex over time is that men become addicted to it and women lose interest in it, though it can happen the other way around too.

The origins of tension in sex

The tension in sex often comes from a deep core belief that this energy is somehow wrong or bad. Thus when we start to feel turned on, we start to contract our muscles against the energy building in our sexual centre. We automatically go into resistance against the sexual energy that is building. When the sexual energy is too strong for the resistance to hold, we let it go in a tension-release orgasm, and the whole sexual encounter is over, or at least has to take a long break.

Tantrics and Taoists understood that over time this kind of sexual act depletes the body's precious reserves of life-force energy. When you are young you may not necessarily feel this loss, but as you age you begin to notice that sexual encounters can drain your energy. The classic situation is one in which the man rolls over and snores after ejaculating, whilst the woman has yet to reach orgasm. Over an extended period of time, tension-release sex can lead to low levels of energy, poor general health and depleted vitality.

There are many solo and couples' practices to undo these habits of contraction and move towards a more relaxed arousal – this is the first stage. The second stage is sublimation, in which you learn to raise the sexual energy up through your body, and there are several techniques.

As sublimation can induce an altered state of bliss it can make you feel quite 'high', and that's a good time to enter meditation. Sometimes the sublimation is so strong that you may not even have to try to meditate, as the bliss simply captures the awareness and the two (bliss and awareness) unite and merge. At some point, however, you will need to ground yourself in some way, perhaps by lying on the floor for a few minutes, to draw the energy back down to Earth before resuming your normal interactions with the outside world.

Sublime sexual energy

Sublimation is the absolute core of Tantric practice. Many people know of Tantra as 'that kind of sex in which you stop ejaculation'. This, however, is a misunderstanding, or at least a misperception. It is not just about stopping ejaculation or tension-release orgasm, it is more importantly about *raising the sexual energy up through the body* or as Osho famously said:

'From sex to superconsciousness.'

Thus the main point is not just to stop ejaculation – that is just one step to facilitate the sublimation of the energy – but to move towards sublimation, and avoiding ejaculation is just one factor to help with this. However you may find it helpful to consider the practice of sublimation from several angles. These include:

Refinement

Sublimation is the process of refining sexual energy. The energy is lifted from its heavier, coarser form – raw sex drive – and transformed into a lighter more refined version – bliss. The spine is like the refinery mechanism. Taoists understood the spine to contain a series of energy pumps that transform the energy as it flows along it. This makes the energy more sublime. Thus you can attain very strong states of spiritual bliss and ecstasy, powered up by raw sexual energy.

Healing

Sexual energy is thought by Taoists to hold our ancestral *chi* (ancestral energy): the codes of the conditioning passed down to us through the generations. This is the karma, or limited patterns, that we came here to heal in this lifetime. Ancestral habits can be very strong and keep us in a limited belief system and so very hard to shake off. However, when we sublimate our sexual energy the energy vibration rises higher and higher, and in these higher states we can shake off old patterns and become free (rather like boiling water in a pan to clear out impurities).

Full-body orgasm

When sexual energy remains localized in the sexual area, you have a tension-release orgasm, as described earlier (*see page 88*). However, when you channel that energy up through the body, it naturally enters a state of full-body orgasm. Not only does the sexual area experience orgasm but also the heart can orgasm (a 'heartgasm') and the brain can orgasm into high states of bliss. In fact, any part of the body or all parts of the body can enter vibration and ecstasy.

Orgasmic prayer

Sublimation leads us into orgasmic prayer. When the sexual energy rises upwards, there can be a very strong experience of expansion. You may frequently move into ecstasy and feel a connection to a higher force. Rather than feeling confined to your separate physical self, you'll expand and feel interconnected to all that is. This can bring waves of gratitude, bliss, ecstasy and an experience of Divine Union – uniting with Existence. This merging with the divine is also sometimes called 'skydancing'.

Moving from contraction to expansion

In Tantra there is the understanding that pure consciousness is unbound, and that our human experience is a contracted state. The more contracted we are, the more we experience separation, pain and suffering. As we expand, we move from feeling separate into feeling interconnected. Our problems seem to disappear as we expand.

*Stress and tension can only exist when
we are in a state of contraction.*

If we can expand then life force and creativity flow through us and we feel like our true soul self here on earth. Tantric orgasm is a practice that shifts us from habitual contracted states into the ability to stay open and expanded. Thus we can shift our whole perception of our life from one of struggle and difficulty to one of feeling expanded and free, creative and limitless. That's a good reason to practise Tantric orgasm!

Transforming negative emotions

Sublimation is not only about raising sexual energy, but also beginning to transform heavier emotions to lighter ones. Heavy feelings might include depression, self-hatred, grief, sadness and so on, and these emotions weigh us down and can make us feel stuck, as they block our *joie de vivre*. Then there are charged emotions such as anger and irritation, which we tend to try to discharge by projecting them onto others, and so negatively impact our relationships.

When we start to practise sublimation, we also sublimate these heavy emotions into lighter ones. This process can affect our entire reality! If you are depressed, then life seems depressing. If you are angry, then life seems annoying. In fact our whole experience of life is largely governed by our inner state. Therefore, if you can uplift and transform these heavy emotions, then your whole reality shifts into a more pleasant and joyful life experience.

Practice: Sublimating emotions

Next time you feel a strong negative emotion, turn your senses inwards for a moment, away from the outside world, by closing your eyes. Notice the energy in your body and how it feels. Relax your contracted muscles so that this energy and sensation can rise upwards towards the crown of your head. Breathe deeply to facilitate the movement of the energy. When you feel the charge of the emotion has shifted, open your eyes and view your world again from this new inner space.

Sexual energy sublimation

Some of the practices of sublimation will be covered in Chapter 14 (*see page 153*); however, there are some preliminary practices that it is recommended to master first – keep practising them until you feel confident:

❖ Bring awareness to the breath. Practice breath meditations for several weeks, until you can shift your state of consciousness through these meditations (*see page 35*).

❖ Learn to become conscious of sexual energy in your body and the sensations that it generates (*see page 123*).

❖ Open the channels of the spine with unaroused sexual energy before raising up sexual energy (*see page 150*). In yoga and qigong this is done by bringing the breath up the spine in meditation.

SUMMARY

❖ To sublimate means to raise energy up in order to experience a higher level of consciousness; this can also bring states of bliss.

❖ Sexual energy can be raised through yoga, qigong or full-body orgasm.

❖ We often have habits of contracting around sexual energy, creating tension that results in an inevitable release of the energy.

❖ In Tantra we practise overcoming these habits to meet sexual energy with expansion.

❖ You can use sublimation to transform heavy or negative emotions.

❖ Sublimation leads to healing and transformation. It is experienced as full-body orgasm and even by some people as a spiritual experience.

Chapter 9
Principle 5: Transfiguration

'When you meet anyone, remember it is a holy encounter. As you see him, you will see yourself... for in him you will find yourself or lose yourself.'

A COURSE IN MIRACLES

Transfiguration is a core part of Tantra and means to see the Divine in something or someone. In other words, to see the truth of who they are: their original innocence. At first, it is something that you practise; however, with experience the Tantric adept aims to achieve a permanent state of transfiguration, in which they see the Divine in and through everything. This is also sometimes called 'enlightenment with the eyes open'.

Tantra is not a solo path of awakening but rather it embraces our interconnectedness, especially through relationships. There is no such enlightenment in Tantra in which one person sits triumphantly in their state of awakening, whilst acting with separation from the people around them. Truth and love go hand in hand in Tantra. To know your own true nature is to know the true nature of everyone, even if they themselves have forgotten. It is through acts of love and forgiveness that we reawaken everyone around us.

Relationship thus becomes a vehicle for awakening. In Tantra we begin to perceive that we are all here to wake each other up. Not in an arrogant holier-than-thou kind of way, but through deep and genuine compassion. When you know the oneness of all beings, you have no choice but to love each person as your own kin. It happens naturally.

Judgement keeps us separate. When we judge others, we are choosing separation over love. Often we judge other people's behaviour as not being in alignment with the highest self. However, in transfiguration we forgo judgement and instead bring compassion and forgiveness. We choose not to identify with the other by their misaligned actions and words, and see their true nature instead. This true nature lies at the source of all actions and words, so it is always possible to perceive it, if we so choose.

In practising transfiguration, we choose to see everyone's true nature, and this serves as a constant reminder to us of our own higher self.

In the presence of an awakened Tantric, others find that they are naturally moved into a state of transfiguration. Many people enjoy this and gravitate towards Tantrics, while others may judge the Tantrics and move away from them. Tantra is not an evangelical path that tries to convert or awaken people; it is more of an open invitation that you choose to gravitate towards.

Transfiguration is non-conditional. You choose to see the divine nature of all beings, whilst honouring their freewill to act as they want to. They may choose to act in their egoic separate self or from their higher self: that is up to them. But the Tantric chooses to see their true nature regardless and treat them as an aspect of God – no matter how they are actually behaving.

Practising transfiguration

Transfiguration can be a choice, it can be an intention and it can also be a practice. You can simply choose to see the divine nature of everyone, even if you don't know exactly what that means at first. Set this as your intention at the start of each day, 'Today I will see the divine nature of all the people that I meet', then go about your day and see what happens.

But the most common way to practise transfiguration is through the eyes. We are trying to change our vision and so we want to see things differently. We are generally raised to look critically at others. We are taught to judge and assess, to categorize and label. These actions all create more of a sense of separateness between them and us.

When we look at extreme cases of anti-transfiguration in the world we can see disastrous results. Racism is one example, and so many times in history this has led to war, hatred and slavery. But even on a less extreme level, we often fall into habits of assessing everyone we meet in a critical way. Instead of seeing oneness, we see separation.

> *With transfiguration, we are*
> *making a different choice. We are*
> *choosing to see things differently.*

Even if we are attached to a particular judgement about someone, we can be open to seeing that person differently. With that openness and choice everything can shift. This shift is the transfiguration. It is not about turning a blind eye to faults, but shifting focus to the true nature of someone – the core of their being, which is connected to the core of your own being. In fact, they are one truth, one love. Thus transfiguration brings the deepest level of connection, which in our hearts we are all seeking.

You can use the following transfiguration practice with anyone, of any gender, as it is non-sexual. However, it is especially helpful for couples to use this practice regularly together. It is common in intimate relationships to fall into habits of anti-transfiguration: to criticize one another and focus on their weak points. So regular transfiguration is like a reminder of your beloved's true nature.

Practice: Transfiguration

Using this practice regularly over time will help you to relate soul to soul rather than personality to personality. This brings depth, respect, honour and sacredness to the relationship, as well as cultivating unconditional love.

1. Sit opposite someone in a comfortable position. You may be on chairs opposite each other, or on two cushions in a cross-legged position. It is best to hold each another's hands, in a relaxed and comfortable way. If you like you can play some relaxing, non-invasive music for this meditation. You may also want to set a timer to ring after 10 minutes.

2. Close your eyes and scan your inner world. Are you relaxed? Breathing deeply? Comfortable? Take a deep breath with a long

drawn-out sigh to relax deeper into this moment. Three deep sighs is usually a good way to begin.

3. When you are ready, open your eyes. You will see the person opposite. If you notice yourself making any judgement of them, offer the judgement up to Highest Consciousness and say, 'I am willing to see this person differently. Please show me this person in Truth.'

4. Now open your heart space. Bring awareness to your chest area and notice how much space there is between your armpits. Use your intention to open this area up. Expand it, as if making space in your heart in which to hold this other person. Breathe into this space, and let it be alive with breath and with love.

5. Look into your partner's eyes and see into their soul. Do not concern yourself with how to do this, just be open to seeing.

6. As you look into their eyes, if you see fear then send it love, as if loving a frightened child. If you see love, then there is nothing to do but meet that love. Dissolve into that love. Love is our true nature. Love is God. God is love.

7. You can sit together for 10 minutes seeing the soul of the other, seeing their divine nature. There is nothing to do but love. If your mind wanders, just come back when you realize. Forgive yourself and return to love.

8. At the end, when the timer bell rings, bring your hands into prayer position. You can bow very slowly towards each other, bowing to the divine within. If you like you can say 'Namaste', which literally means 'I bow to the divine in you'.

Integrate this experience by closing your eyes and sitting in silence for a few moments. At this point you are not touching your partner, but have returned to your own space. You may want to set a second timer for 5–10 minutes of solo meditation.

SUMMARY

- ❖ Transfiguration means to see the truth of who someone is, rather than see the transient passing moods, words, beliefs or other expressions they might have.

- ❖ Transfiguration is a choice we can make in daily life, but we can also practise it.

- ❖ Transfiguration is a shift from judgement to love.

- ❖ When we focus too much on the characteristics of separation we can develop racism, sexism and other forms of hatred. This is called anti-transfiguration.

Chapter 10

The Principles of Tantric Healing

'Tantra trusts in your body. Tantra trusts in your senses. Tantra trusts in your energy. Tantra trusts in you – in total. Tantra does not deny anything but transforms everything.'

Oshо

Tantra is a path of healing, or becoming whole. In one way we can see every aspect of Tantric practice having a healing effect. This is due to the unifying principle in Tantra, which allows opposites to merge into oneness (*see page 82*). We become sick or out of balance when we start to split ourselves into pieces. We feel harmonious and complete when we heal those splits.

In nature, reality can be seen as being made up of light and dark in a continuous dance together. In the daytime the light comes out, in the night nature falls into darkness. There is always at least some darkness in the light, for example under rocks and inside caves it is dark even in full daylight hours. There is also light in the darkness, whether that is the moon or the stars. So light and dark are not separate, but interconnected and in constant motion together.

In Taoism the light and dark are called 'yin' (dark) and 'yang' (light) and the famous yin-yang symbol shows the two in continuous flow into one another, with the opposite embedded at the core of each. Together they make the whole.

The yin-yang symbol

Nature doesn't judge light over dark or dark over light. Both are needed to create this universe. The continuous dance of light and dark is a natural process. By contemplating the movements of light and dark in nature, we often come into connection to Source – the creative force behind all of existence, which is also known as the Divine and some may call 'God'. In Taoism it is called quite simply 'the Tao' and in Tantra it may be referred to as '*Annutara*', or sometimes as Shiva (but this is slightly confusing as Shiva is used to describe the masculine principle as well – *see page 12*).

However, take a look around human reality and you'll tend to find less harmony than in nature. Suddenly we find a struggle between light and dark. We find that we have to choose which to identify with, because in human reality there is so often a split between them. Either you are angelic, obedient and good. You wear pretty clothes and say all the right things. Or you are dark, physical and rebellious. You wear black or Gothic clothing: something that shows what a rebel you are. You hang out in dangerous places and look as menacing as possible.

Reflected in this, we find the sexual-spiritual split. You can be sexual if you are rebellious and bad. But if you want to be angelic and holy and socially acceptable, you had better keep sex within the confines of a marriage or a steady relationship, or not at all! And thus we have developed conflicts within our selves and our societies. We have created painful splits. We feel torn between choices. We may identify with those who appear to have made the same choice as us, and we judge those who choose the opposite (often secretly longing to be like them!). This is the human condition!

Many people express this split personality through having a public face like a mask, and a shadow that they keep hidden away. In public, they may display all of the characteristics that they believe will gain them acceptance into their peer group. In private, they act out or suppress all of the aspects that they fear will have them forever condemned or rejected.

We can only be free when we are able to live beyond the confines of our own self-limiting identities.

We form these assumptions as we grow up; they are pieced together from the messages we received from our family, teachers and friends. We try to fit ourselves into the identities that we think will gain us acceptance. Every human has a basic need for love and acceptance, and one of our core fears is rejection and abandonment. At one point in our evolutionary development, for example, if the tribe rejected us, we would surely die. So no wonder we developed such strong behaviours to try to fit in.

There is a certain survival advantage to these developed behaviours, for example we are accepted into the crowd, taken in by our tribe. But at a great cost: our authenticity. How can we be total, be whole, be complete if we are censoring ourselves? How can we feel at ease, if we are hiding certain parts of our nature? How can we relax into our being, if we are trying to be something or someone to earn acceptance and approval? In this situation, the whole time you have to live in fear of being 'found out'.

Tantra aims to support us back to totality. Back to our true nature. To naturalness. It is a healing journey, in which we reclaim the split-off parts of ourselves and bring them back to unity. We move away from our cultured and conditioned self, and return to our authentic nature. This often involves shining the light of awareness into our shadows and hidden parts. And then creating spaces of love and acceptance for all of those rejected pieces. As we reclaim the shadows, the masks of protection fall away.

Principles of Tantric healing

It is helpful to understand the main Tantric principles of healing before you embark on a healing journey. In Neo-Tantra (*see page 19*), there has been a fusion of Tantra with psychotherapy and the following principles are found in many Tantric healing methods:

Light of awareness

Bring the shadows into the light of awareness, and the masks will naturally fall away. This is because the masks were simply there for protection. Once a person feels safe to own their shadow side, they will release the protection naturally.

No judgement

Our shadow self needs to be witnessed without judgement by others. We hide it because we are afraid that we will be rejected; therefore when we feel witnessed and accepted, a great healing occurs.

Love and acceptance

Healing is the application of love to the places that are suffering. Healing is not about fixing someone, but about having compassion for the suffering that each of us carries. If someone is trying to fix you, this can even block the process of healing. However, love and acceptance is the balm that heals all.

Energy flow

We have to allow the accompanying emotions/energy to flow without censoring them or restraining them. This is an important part of healing. In Tantra sometimes a method will be used to allow the energy to flow within the body, as emotions are understood to be the result of energy flow and energy blockages. The chakra system is often used in Tantra to understand energy flow in more detail.

Tantra 101

'Chakra' means wheel and is well known in classical yogic theory. It is an understanding that energy flows through the body and that there are certain vortices of this energy through the centre of the human body. These energetic centres are the locations of particular transformations that can happen on our healing journey as we move from contraction to expansion and from fear to love.

Root chakra, *muladhara*: Located at the perineum, our 'root'. When energy is blocked here we can experience fears around survival and fear of being in a body. When this chakra is opened and free flowing, we feel a lot of vitality, supported by life and a deep sense of embodiment.

Second chakra, *svadhisthana*: Located above the pubic bone. If energy gets blocked here we may have difficulty experiencing pleasure, and instead feel guilt and shame. Or we may develop very unconscious sexual expression or a tendency to use drugs and alcohol. When the energy is freely flowing then we feel sensual in a natural way, and pleasure is relaxed in our being.

Third chakra, *manipura*: Located above the navel. If energy is blocked here we may have problems with anger, frustration and violence, either inwardly or externally expressed. People may feel blocked in their passion, instead feeling dull and frustrated. When the energy is free flowing then we feel passionate about life, alive and focused without control.

Fourth chakra, *anahata*: Located in the centre of the chest. If energy is blocked here then we feel separate from other people. This can have several forms including loneliness, depression, hatred, resentment and other forms of lack of love. When this chakra is blocked people may have too few intimate relationships or a lot of conflict within their relationships. When the energy is freely flowing, we feel loving, kind and compassionate.

Fifth chakra, *vishuddha*: Located in the throat. If energy is blocked here then we feel a lack of trust in spontaneity. We may have no creative expression and find it hard to express ourselves. When the energy is flowing, we feel able to express creatively and spontaneously.

Sixth chakra, *ajna*: Located in between and slightly above the eyebrows. If energy is blocked here then we feel narrow-minded, trapped in limiting beliefs and concepts. If it is free flowing then we see the divine in and through everything. It is as if we can see the interconnectedness of all things.

Seventh chakra, *sahasrara*: Located at the crown of the head. If energy is blocked here then we feel separate from Existence, just an isolated individual. If this chakra is open, then we feel interconnected with the universe, like a ray of one same sun.

Integration

In order that the process is completed, the person will need to have some integration following an emotional release. This may be meditation, silence or physical holding. This helps to bring the system back to centre and allow the body–mind system to complete the process.

Many people overlook this stage, but it is a vital step in the process for completion of healing. It is integration that allows us to merge expansive experiences back into our daily life, so that we can take something long-term from passing experiences. Without proper integration people are sometimes left feeling confused after a healing experience.

Holding space

Healing is frequently undertaken with someone holding space for the recipient (sometimes called a healer or facilitator). This person is there to witness the shadows of the recipient, and also to act as a sort of container when emotions are released. The capacity to hold space is a direct result of all of the inner work that the healer has done. The more healing a person has been through, the more capacity they have to facilitate for another.

A good space holder has a strong presence about them. If you feel relaxed and safe in someone's presence, then that person is a good space holder for you. If you are looking for a facilitator or healer then trust your instinctual wisdom; if you naturally feel like opening up, then this is a good space holder for you. You should never need to feel pushed to open up.

In Tantric relationships, the capacity of each partner to hold space for one another is a really important factor. In fact it is not about choosing a partner with a list of certain qualities or attributes, but being drawn towards the person in whose presence you feel safe enough to open up. This brings a naturally healing quality to a Tantric relationship.

Encounter with a Tantric man

I will never forget one of the first times I encountered a man who really knew how to hold space. I was in a retreat centre (a good place to find such men) and my immediate feeling when we were introduced was that I was not interested in him – after all he was shorter than me, and in my eyes that was a big no-no.

However, I did notice his gaze upon me. It was not piercing or intimidating, but he was just so present. Even from right across a large table, I felt myself shift in his presence. I felt seen.

Later he grabbed me for a dance across the restaurant. No one else was dancing. But he whizzed me around and made me giggle like a teenager. My guard was coming down. He danced me right off the dance floor and onto the beach.

As I spent time with this man, there were moments when I opened up and then others in which I'd suddenly feel fear and close up. He never pushed me, but simply saw me, held me in his presence. If I went into fear and contraction, he would look at me lovingly and just be present until he saw me relax and open again. I felt myself opening to deeper and deeper layers of my being simply by being in his presence.

Needless to say, we eventually got together. We had a wonderful relating journey, with a lot of love and expansion. There was a lot of healing for both of us, within the space we held for one another. We dropped many old patterns of defence from old relationship experiences, and opened up again to our loving natures. In all of our time together, he never ceased to hold an incredible space for me. I always remember him with a warm glow in my heart.

The next section of this book is experiential, and this is your opportunity to put the Tantra principles into practice. It is designed to guide you on your own journey into an exploration of Tantra. You can embark on this journey alone, or together with a partner or friend.

SUMMARY

❖ Light and dark are part of nature's cycles, and in nature they are interconnected. When they become split by the human mind, then we start to feel an inner split, an inner conflict. This often manifests as outer conflicts.

❖ We form a shadow side when we hide parts of ourselves out of fear and shame. If we think society will reject us then we try to hide those parts.

❖ We cannot be authentic and real if we are trying to hide parts of ourselves.

❖ Tantric healing is about forgiving and loving those parts, and embracing the totality.

❖ Healing principles used in Tantra are to bring the shadow to the light of awareness, let those aspects be witnessed without judgement, apply love, move energy and integrate the healing.

❖ The principle of holding space is when one person witnesses another's wounds without judgement, catalysing the other person's healing.

❖ If lovers hold space for one another, then healing becomes a part of their relationship.

Part III
THE TANTRIC JOURNEY

*'The search for love is but the
honest searching out of everything
that interferes with love.'*

A Course in Miracles

Chapter 11

Opening Your Heart

*'When the power of love overcomes the
love of power, the world will know peace.'*

JIMI HENDRIX

So, you have found out about the history, the elements and the principles of Tantra, and now you feel ready to start to imbibe it. Tantra is a journey, an embodied experience, and therefore it is experience and practice that opens us up to this path.

Where to begin? Tantra is a path of the heart and so this is a good place to begin. If you don't have an open heart, then all of the other practices you do may be coming from a place of trying to 'fix' yourself or make yourself 'more Tantric' and run the risk of coming from ego-self instead of nourishing your higher self.

In opening the heart, we begin with self-love. If all of our actions come from a loving place, then we will be walking on the path of love.

Listening to your heart

Some people are drawn to Tantra to heal their hearts. Many people experience painful emotions around love, such as a broken heart, rejection, loneliness or disappointment. Not just from romantic experiences, but from childhood, family and friendships that have created disconnection. This kind of pain can tempt us to close down our hearts, protecting us from feeling the pain but also preventing us from feeling love.

Some may have been taught to keep their hearts closed down from such an early age that although they don't experience much emotional pain they feel shut off from life and from love. This may be experienced as feeling cold, and life may appear to be loveless.

*Keeping our hearts closed down may feel
safe, but there is a deep aching within.*

When we are not giving and receiving love in our lives, we feel a deep longing inside. Of course, many people make themselves too busy to feel this. You may wake in the middle of the night and feel the longing, or awaken in the morning to a deep ache for more love. If this arises for you, try not to push it way and get busy trying to distract yourself. Notice if you reach for your smartphone or leap out of bed to make coffee... and instead just take a deep breath and try to be present with the longing.

Such a longing is actually the start of the heart trying to open up. It is not a problem we have to fix, but a calling we have to listen to.

Practice: Listening to your heart

If we don't listen to our callings, sometimes life sends us louder and louder calls, until we hear. Why wait until life brings you an accident, a painful breakup or a midlife crisis? Use the following practice to help you listen to your heart's deepest longings, and to bring yourself back onto the path of love, your true path.

1. Sit in a quiet space where you won't be disturbed.

2. Place your hands flat over your heart, as if holding it in your hands.

3. Take a deep breath into your heart area and let out the breath with a big 'ahhh' sigh. Try a few of these, letting your heart release tension and defences.

4. Now begin to look down into your heart space in the centre of your chest (this is the heart chakra rather than the physical organ, the place you instinctively point to when you say 'me' – *see page 106*).

5. Begin to breathe right in and out of this space. Feel your chest rise and fall under your hands.

6. Notice the sensations awakening in the area. Do not try to label or analyse them, or judge them as either good or bad. Just notice them.

7. Begin to listen in to your heart for any feeling of longing.

8. If you find some longing, just bring breath to it. Let it exist. Let it be felt. Let it be heard.

9. Sit for several breaths just listening in this way. You can gently smile down to all that you find in your heart, no matter what it is. No judgement. Nothing to push away. Give your heart the time and space to feel whatever is alive inside of it.

10. When you have finished, put your hands into a prayer position and make a bow to your beautiful heart.

How does the heart heal?

Remember that the healing of the heart is not a problem to be fixed. In fact the truth is that the universe has our highest interests at heart. The universe is generous, like a parent (hence God is often described as the Divine Father or Divine Mother). There is so much love wanting to be given to us. Sometimes we don't believe that because we cannot feel it. But the truth is that we don't feel it because we are not letting it in, not because it isn't there. So many great spiritual avatars have told us over and over again that the Truth is good news and the ultimate reality is love.

So what is in the way?

We are! All of the defences that we have built in response to fears (that were actually not true) create walls that stop the love flowing in. So when it comes to healing the heart, we are actually just learning to receive love. We are remembering how it is to receive, just as a newborn baby receives its parents' love without any guilt.

Receiving love means we become tremendously vulnerable. It is a process of letting down our guard, dropping our defences, and being utterly soft and receptive. This is because we have learned from a distorted world that it is not safe. We have come to believe we will be rejected or abandoned or mocked if we become that vulnerable, because we learned from people who had their defences up and were not comfortable in the presence of love.

To heal the heart we have to relearn to be as vulnerable and open as a baby.

It is essential for us to move out of unloving environments and relationships, which reinforce that it is unsafe to open the heart. In spirituality there is a wonderful word, '*sangha*', which means a spiritual community. This is your tribe of friends who are also choosing to awaken and heal. Being surrounded by these people will start to make it safe to open your heart once more.

Exercise: Choosing supportive friends, lovers and communities

Notice how your feel in someone's company or in a particular community and take a note of your answers:

❖ Are you relaxed and able to be authentic or do you feel as though you have to put on a bit of an act?

❖ What happens when you express deep emotions or vulnerable stories with this person? How do they respond? Do you feel safe?

❖ Does your heart open in their presence?

❖ Do you feel violated when you have expressed something vulnerable? Or do you feel deeply accepted no matter what you express to them?

❖ How do they express their deepest hearts? Do they share their vulnerability with you?

❖ Do you feel safe? Can you trust them not to tell others what you have shared? Can you trust them not to talk behind your back? How safe do you feel?

❖ Do you feel a natural flow of trust with them?

The good news is that you don't need to find the perfect lover to heal your heart! In fact it can be a better idea to find friends or a spiritual community that nourishes your heart instead. Let your heart heal in that loving environment, and then when you are ready you will attract a lover who is ready to meet you there.

Opening to self-love

We hear a lot about self-love in the world of healing and self-development. But what does it mean and how do we develop it?

Self-love is not about narcissistic self-adoration, as this would only create more ego-self, and thus separation from others and an attitude of 'I am better than you'. Self-love is actually about having compassion for the wounds that we carry, and holding those wounds in a space of love to support their healing.

We all have wounds that we gather along the way in this life. These are often the result of being handed down other people's unhealed wounds. So there may have been times when your parents were not acting from perfect love, or when you were bullied at school. Whatever the source of the wounds, they are from times when there was a lack of love. And so they are calling for love and your heart is all that is needed.

The heart is an alchemist. It transforms pain into love. In Tantra we do not need to avoid pain, but to take it into an open heart and allow this transformation to happen. Having an open heart is not about pretending to be all fluffy and loving. It is actually deeply courageous, as you face pain, yours and others, and allow it to be felt so deeply that the alchemy of love can happen.

In the current world in which we live, where there is mass pain, war, conflict and suffering, we need those courageous hearts to show up. Self-love doesn't stop at feeling compassion for yourself: it starts there. Once the heart is open you'll remember your connection with all of life; and from that place realize that all pain is your pain.

An open heart dissolves the illusion of separation.

The journey of opening the heart begins with reawakening your heart's sensitivity. When the heart is open it feels touched by life, it feels moved. You will feel touched by loving situations and you will feel touched by unloving situations. The heart is like a sixth sense: it senses love and lovelessness. So to open your heart, you have to be willing to let go of being 'cool' and allow yourself to be sensitive again (*see also page 58*). You have to be willing to feel all that is going on in this world, no matter how ugly it is, and breathe it in. You are a part of all of it.

Practice: Atisha's Heart Meditation for self-love

The following practice is one of the classic meditations for opening the heart to self-love and is named after the teacher Atisha from Tibet. It is very close to the technique found in Tibetan Tantric Buddhism known as 'Tonglen Meditation'. It is very simple, and yet very powerful, as it involves the alchemy of breathing in pain, directly into the heart, and breathing out love.

1. Sit somewhere where you will not be disturbed and be comfortable. It is best to sit in a way that allows your chest to feel open, so check that you are not slouched.

2. Take a few minutes to tune in and listen to your heart. Place your hands over your chest to help bring awareness here.

3. Once you feel your heart space, begin to feel any areas in your life where you have pain or suffering. It could be physical, emotional or even existential (the pain of being alive).

4. Take one area at a time. Take a few moments to feel the pain. Then breathe it into your heart with a deep inhale. Let your heart be touched.

5. As you exhale, send a wave of love to that area in your life – like a soft mist of loving vibrations.

6. Continue to inhale pain and exhale love to this one situation for a few breaths. You may notice a subtle shift happening within.

7. When you feel complete, scan for another area of your life that has pain and repeat the breathing alchemy there.

8. At the end, bring awareness back to your heart and listen to it once more. Smile to any tenderness that you find there. Become present with how it feels to have an open and sensitive heart.

Atisha's Heart Meditation with a partner

1. Sit opposite a partner or friend.

2. Close your eyes and then both of you should spend 5 minutes doing your own internal Atisha's Heart Meditation (see above).

3. Ring a little bell or use a timer to let you know when to open your eyes.

4. As you look into your partner's eyes, look into their heart. Inhale and imagine you are taking all of their pain and suffering right into your heart. You do not need to try to analyse what their pain might be or know their story. Just look into their eyes and breathe in their pain.

5. As you exhale, send a soft wave of love on your breath to their heart.

6. Continue for 10 minutes together.

7. Close your eyes, hold your heart in your hands and take 5 minutes more to listen to your heart.

Atisha's Heart Meditation for world suffering

This can be done at the end of either of the above meditations or as a standalone practice. I often do this when I read about world tragedies or see the news. I know a man who has travelled around the world to places where mass suffering has occurred such as former concentration camps and war zones. He sits and does Atisha's Heart Meditation in these places. Never underestimate the power of your own heart to heal.

1. Close your eyes and listen to your heart for a few minutes.

2. Now inhale the pain and suffering of the world. It may be a general sense of pain and suffering, or there could be a specific incident that you heard about on the news.

3. Exhale, sending a wave of love back to those places.

4. Let yourself be touched – you may even start to cry during this meditation as the heart's protection melts down and the sensitivity reawakens. Have the courage to feel.

5. Take a few minutes to breathe in pain and breathe out love.

6. At the end, bring awareness back to your heart and listen to it.

7. You can end the meditation with your hands in prayer position and make a bow to the healing power of love.

An open heart is the foundation of Tantra

It is advised to keep up a regular Heart Meditation practice throughout all your Tantric exploration because the energies you'll be accessing are very strong and powerful. Power itself is neutral, but it can be used in positive or negative ways. If we use power to support the ego-self, we will only create more separation and pain in our lives. When this power is aligned with love then we will powerfully accelerate our spiritual path in the most heartfelt direction, the direction towards peace.

Tantra 101

Regular practice could be daily if you really want to focus on opening your heart, or you may choose to practise whenever you sense that you are not feeling so much love in your life. You can download guided meditations for the heart at: ShashiSolluna.com/Tantric-Tools

SUMMARY

❖ Make a commitment to listen to your heart.

❖ The heart opens easiest when it feels safe. You can create safety yourself but it's also a good idea to choose loving environments where you feel naturally open.

❖ The alchemy of the heart is to transform pain into love and, as we open our heart, we can heal our inner pain and also the pain of those with whom we're connected. It is not us doing the healing, but love itself.

❖ It is not so much about cultivating love as it is about healing all that stands in the way of love.

❖ Having an open heart is central to Tantra, thus it is worth taking your time to practice heart-opening meditations until you can really feel your heart is open.

Chapter 12
Sexual Healing

'For man and woman to make love beautifully and divinely requires a fundamental change in the penis and the vagina; or more specifically in the part of the brain that controls them.'

<small>BARRY LONG</small>

Once the heart is open and we have developed a higher level of consciousness, we are ready to start on the rest of the Tantric journey. An open heart can create a space that feels safe in which to open up. Such a space is essential if healing is to be smooth and without the risk of creating more trauma. When we feel loved and accepted, we spontaneously begin to enter the healing process.

Often we begin the sexual arts with a process of purification and healing. If your pot is full when you come to the spring, you cannot take in any of the waters. First you need to tip out the old stagnant water and then you'll have plenty of space to receive the new waters.

In order to receive the Tantra essence and energy, we often need to clear out some old beliefs and conditioning. We need to find all the parts we have buried deep inside ourselves out of shame and guilt and fear, and let them be seen and thus freed. This process is part of our Tantric healing.

Healing from the roots

In Tantra it is common to work from the base upwards. This is because sexual repression and conditioning cause a lot of energy to become trapped in the sexual centre. We cannot become alive and live to our full potential if our sexual-creative energy is trapped at the roots. In classical Tantra, they say that the kundalini energy (potent creative energy) is coiled up in the base of the spine. If it remains here it creates a world of illusion. But if it is released and rises up the spine, one can become enlightened and enlivened.

What this means is that we have a huge potential of creative life-force energy but repression can keep it blocked, leaving us feeling dull and lacking in vitality. Tantra acknowledges that there is no way to avoid going into the depths and clearing out the blockages:

*We simply need to enter our sexual
Pandora's box in order to release the
energy. This is the sexual healing.*

However it is not just about liberating sexual energy and being taken over by desire! In Tantra there is also a whole system of raising the sexual energy so that we can channel this energy into higher centres, such as opening the heart to more love and opening the mind to higher states of consciousness. We can still enjoy our sexual desire, but we are not ruled by it.

Once the lower energy can rise up and reconnect to love and spirit, then we feel whole, aligned and integrated. This brings a feeling of easy authenticity that so many of us yearn for with no idea how to attain it.

> *Once we are healed and whole, we reunite*
> *with our spiritual nature, which is totality.*

Sexual conditioning

We often think of our sexuality as being a natural function. Yet we are unique animals in that we have developed a culture that has judged and manipulated sexuality in so many ways. Though we all came from sex in the first place, almost every culture in the world has a surprising number of hang-ups about it.

The Taoist Sexual Arts have a wonderful intention to heal by transforming our sexual cultural conditioning back into our sexual nature. The Taoists see sexual energy as coming from Nature herself, and to allow this energy to flow freely again we need to become natural again. This involves releasing any inner judgement patterns that make us distort and control our sexuality.

> *Tantra transforms your sexual conditioning*
> *back into your sexual nature.*

Suppression, rebellion and healing

For some reason, we have evolved a fear of sexuality and the energy behind it. This fear has led to many different forms of judgement and suppression of sexuality. In some cultures we instil fear, guilt and shame into our children for their own natural sexual feelings. This is the beginning of the journey of suppression.

In Tantric healing we begin to undo those blocks so that our natural energy can run freely again. However, this powerful energy does need to be held, rather than running wild and creating havoc in our lives. Rather than hold it with restrictions and limitations, we can begin to hold it with the power of our awareness and the gentleness of our love. As we build awareness, we can let down our guard and release our blocks.

Exercise: Healing shadow desires

A powerful way to heal a shadow is to bring it into the light of awareness. It is especially healing to have someone else witness your shadows without judging or rejecting you. In Tantra this is called 'holding space' (*see also page xvii*). You could do this exercise with your lover or a friend, as it works by exchange so both of you can participate both ways. You will need a timer, such as on a smartphone.

1.   Find a private space where you will not be interrupted and turn off your phone. Agree to keep this exercise confidential, as it is essential to create safe space, and to 'hold space' for each other by listening without commenting or reacting. Your intention is to listen deeply to what the other is saying as they share.

2.   Sit opposite each other, fully facing one another. Decide who will share first.

3.   Start with eyes closed, taking a few deep breaths to still your inner being.

4. Open your eyes and take 3 minutes to look in each other's eyes without saying a single word. Keep breathing deeply and let your heart space (the space between your armpits) be relaxed.

5. The listening partner sets the intention to be open to listen without judgement or reaction.

6. Now the first person gets to share their shadow desires. It can be anything – sexual desires, physical longings, heart yearnings, etc. What desires do you feel a bit ashamed of? What have you suppressed or kept hidden? Use a timer and give yourself 8 minutes.

7. After sharing, put your hands in a prayer position and simply say 'thank you' to each other.

8. Now exchange roles.

9. After sharing, put your hands in a prayer position and simply say 'thank you' to each other again.

10. Close your eyes and sit in silent meditation for 8 minutes.

11. When you have both finished, try to avoid commenting on each other's sharing. In this way, you continue to hold the space.

Healing sexual conditioning

One of the intentions in Tantra is to move from sexual conditioning to sexual nature: a relaxed open relationship with your sexuality and sexual energy. Our conditioning is the collection of learned patterns or rebellious responses to the messages about sexuality we received as we grew up.

It is important to realize that conditioning may be obedient or it may be rebellious, as sometimes we think we have healed our conditioning just by developing the opposite behaviour. But a rebel is still responding to the conditioning and thus still controlled by it. To truly heal we have to move beyond obedience and rebellion and find our authenticity.

Investigating sexual conditioning

As part of Tantric healing it is helpful to consider the messages you have received about sexuality, relationships and gender. These messages may have been verbal, but often come through demonstration and experience. For example, your mother may never have said 'dressing in sexy clothes is dangerous', but if she tensed up when you dressed a certain way, you will have picked up the message anyway.

If we don't gain consciousness of what messages we are carrying, we may act out behaviour that is controlled by this conditioning or rebel against it. Thus we are not completely free or authentic. To return to our sexual nature, we can take some time to explore what messages control us and let them go.

Exercise: Understanding the messages

Take some time and space to yourself, get a notepad and pen (somehow this has a therapeutic value that using a computer or tablet does not have), and turn off your phone. This process is a self-investigation, an opportunity to bring some light into your depths and your unconscious layers.

Please note that this is not about blaming your parents or teachers. Forgiveness is the best way to become free. So if during your investigation you recognize some uncomfortable patterns that you have inherited from someone, remember that they too suffered from these limiting beliefs, and give them your compassion and forgiveness.

If at any point you feel upset or disturbed, simply stop writing and close your eyes. Notice any sensation inside your body and use your breath to make space for it. Allow yourself to witness it fully. If any emotions arise, let them flow.

OK, let's begin.

❖   What messages did you receive about sexuality from your mother? What did she embody herself? How did she express it, if at all? How did she react to sexuality?

❖   Now repeat the same with your father.

❖   What messages were you given about your gender and the opposite gender?

❖   What messages did you receive from religious organizations about sexuality?

❖   What messages did you receive through your formal education about sexuality?

❖   What did all of your friends and siblings express about sexuality? When you all started to enter puberty, what was the general attitude like? What sources of information did you seek?

❖   What message did the media give you? Magazines, books, movies or porn?

❖   Did you receive any harmful or abusive teachings about sexuality or gender? Did any behaviours shown to you, or acted out on you, bring you unconscious messages? If you were going to put those messages into words, what would they say?

❖   Were there any conflicting messages? For example, the magazines told you to be sexy but the priests told you to be demure. Write down any conflicts.

❖   Was there anyone who inspired you as a child? What positive messages did you receive and from whom? Who were your positive role models? What was the most uplifting inspiration and what do you think was the highest level of sexual expression that you witnessed?

❖   Take 5 minutes just to write anything else that may be flowing. Don't think about it, just allow yourself to write what comes.

Afterwards, sit back and close your eyes. Notice any energy or sensation inside your body. Do not judge, label or suppress any sensation. Just simply observe and allow. If any sensation feels intense, take a big breath and let your breath flood the area with the sensation. Let the breath create space for the sensation.

Partner version

If you have a lover or good friend with whom you are on your Tantric journey, you can do this exercise together. Take your time to answer the questions on your own, in your own notepads, without discussion. Then sit in front of each other and take turns to share a summary of your findings. Just as in the previous exercise for healing shadow desires (see page 126), when one partner talks the other one listens, there is no need to pass comment on the other person's sharing. Make an agreement field to keep everything absolutely confidential so that it is a safe and held space.

Sexual healing meditations

After you have investigated your conditioning, you can use a healing meditation to begin to shift the energy in your sexual organs.

Why do we need to move energy?

Once upon a time you were born with free-flowing energy but, as you received messages that made you feel guilty about this energy, you began to try and control and suppress it. So to heal, we want to get that energy flowing freely once more.

The Taoist path has many great practices for healing sexual energy. A foundational meditation in Taoism is the 'Inner Smile'. By smiling to your energy, the energy feels safe to flow (energy is alive and contains its own intelligence). To smile to parts of ourselves can gently undo the damage from all of the times we were chastised, criticized or reprimanded. The 'Inner Smile' meditation is very gentle, and yet regular practice can have very deep effects over time.

Practice: Taoist 'Inner Smile' meditation

This works by bringing softness and acceptance to our sexual energy to help undo any blame and guilt we have accumulated.

1. Sit in a comfortable position where you won't be disturbed.

2. Imagine that the sun has just come out after a long period of grey rainy weather – remember that feeling of joy! Lift your forehead just a few centimetres, as if turning your face to the sun, and smile to that warmth and light.

3. Now inhale and drink that warm light into the point between your eyebrows and exhale with a sigh into your brain. Feel the warmth flooding your brain and relaxing your mind.

4. Repeat this breath a few times, relaxing your mind and thoughts. Let the warmth melt away any hard thinking patterns.

5. Return awareness to the sun you are imagining in front of you, and this time inhale it in through the mid-eyebrow and exhale into your heart. Let your heart breathe for a few breaths. Let the warm smiling energy melt away any hardened places around your heart and chest area.

6. When your heart feels soft and more open, lift your gaze to the sun again. This time when you inhale you will inhale all the way down to your sex centre. Exhale with a big sigh and relax the sex organs and pelvis.

7. With concurrent inhales imagine you are drinking the warm sunlight energy all the way down to your sex. Exhale, expanding and relaxing the whole sexual area. Continue for several breaths until you feel a noticeable relaxation in this area.

8. Then remain focused on the sexual area. Smile down to your sexual centre. Like a parent smiling to a child, smile to anything you feel or sense there right now. You might feel some bubbling active energy, or perhaps the area feels a bit quieter. You have nothing to change: just keep smiling to your sexual area and breathing with your whole pelvic region.

9. Place your hands over your sexual area, as if holding your sexual organs. This will bring even more energy and awareness to this region.

10. Allow anything to arise. You may feel emotions or tears: just allow them. Or you may not feel so much, which can be frustrating. Be patient and loving with yourself, Rome was not built in a day, and Tantric healing is a journey! If you do not feel so much then focus on your breathing, taking deeper and fuller breaths. It is the breath that will reawaken the sensations.

11. Keep coming back to the smile. It might seem simple, but it is the smile that heals all of the times that someone frowned at your natural energy and expression or condemned it. There is a biochemical shift in the body when we smile.

12. After a meditation period of 10–45 minutes (build up over time), take a moment to integrate sex, love and spirit. Do this by feeling the sensations in your sex centre, the sensations in your heart centre and the awareness in your mind. Simply become aware of those three areas and feel them interconnected at your core. Inhale from your root at the perineum (between your genitals and anus) up to your crown, and exhale from your crown to your perineum. This is an integration meditation that harmonizes the three areas.

13. When you feel aligned and integrated, bring your hands into prayer position at your heart and make a bow to your sexual energy.

Another powerful Taoist meditation for healing involves taking a genital sun bath. This is a very simple meditation and involves exposing your genitals for a few minutes to the sunlight. This is not about getting a suntan, but about bringing those parts usually hidden away into the light.

You may experience extreme resistance to this exercise. Even reading about it may have you squirming in your seat! This is just the result of being conditioned to keep these parts hidden away. Countries with a more open attitude to nudity tend also to have a more relaxed attitude to sexuality. It is going to be very hard to be sexually open if you are ashamed of your body and sexual organs.

Practice: Genital sun bath

Choose a place where you can be in the sunlight where you won't offend other people – perhaps a private garden or balcony, or even in front of a window when the sun is shining in. Alternatively, you can visit a naturist beach, if you live near one. It's vital not to do this practice in a place where you could be told off, as this will just add more conditioning and shame! Also of course avoid very strong sunlight, just as you would with sunbathing. This skin is very tender and delicate so don't expose it for any longer than 3–5 minutes.

What is important in this meditation is not the act of the sun reaching your skin, but your awareness of your inner process during the practice. Watch for resistance and contraction, such as tightening your muscles and holding your breath. If you notice these, just take a deep breath and see if you can relax a little.

1. Start by wrapping a towel or sarong round your hips, and then create a sacred space in your chosen secluded spot (*see page 52*).

2. Lie on your back with your knees bent and drop open your sarong/towel.

3. Open your legs wide enough to let in the light. If you feel very open, then you could even drop your knees to the side in a 'butterfly' position, exposing your sexual area even more. However, if you find this exercise challenging, then just start with bent knees.

4. Take a few deep breaths, as if breathing into your genitals.

5. Feel the sensations of the light and warmth on your skin and sexual organs. How does it feel? Can you feel the warmth? Just notice without judgement.

6. Check inside for contractions and tension and just use deep breathing to relax even more.

7. Imagine the sunlight is the light of pure consciousness landing on your sexual organs, healing away past shame. If you like you can add an internal affirmation such as 'my sexual organs are a part of nature' or 'my sexual organs are innocent'. And of course smile to your sexual organs. See what helps you feel open and relaxed.

8. After 3–5 minutes, cover up again with your towel or sarong and stretch your legs out flat on the floor. Take a few deep breaths and let your body relax and integrate the experience.

This may seem like a simple meditation, but a few minutes every day can really begin to clear old shame and rebuild your relationship to your body and sexual organs. If you happen to be in a country and season with a lack of sunshine, then you can set up a desk-lamp pointing towards your genitals and do this meditation.

The next practice follows on from the last and is about seeing yourself and bearing witness to your genitals. Again, the idea often seems a bit ridiculous when you first hear it. But just as shining a light on your genitals can heal shame, so too can being seen and witnessed as you are: in your innocence.

Practice: Genital revelation

This practice can be especially powerful for women, as they do not get so see their sexual organs in the way that men do theirs. But even for a man, to just sit and meditate upon the genitals is not something we are encouraged to do in normal circumstances!

1. Place a full-length mirror against a wall with a yoga mat or blanket laid out in front of it.

2.   Make sure your room is private and you will not be interrupted.

3.   Play some soft and relaxing music, and lie down naked on your back, propped up on your elbows or on a big pile of cushions, so you can see in the mirror.

4.   Take a moment to see yourself as a lover would see you, from an angle you do not usually get to see! If judgements arise, offer them up to the Highest Consciousness and ask that you can see your true innocence. Take a deep breath, relax and release any negative thoughts with your exhale.

5.   Begin to focus in upon your genitals. Lift them up if you are a man, and see from different angles. If you are a woman, open up your labia (the vaginal lips) and take a look at the different layers. Look from as neutral a perspective as you can, as if seeing for the first time. Come with an attitude of curiosity and wonder. Keep checking in on your breath and make sure you are breathing deeply.

6.   After your exploration, close your eyes and watch what is happening within yourself. Can you feel energy moving? Do you feel relaxed and expanded, or tight and contracted? Do you feel turned on? Do you feel disturbed? Just observe and breathe and be aware.

This practice can help us to come into a comfortable and relaxed attitude with our own nudity and our own genitals. If we feel ashamed or disconnected, then we will not be able to share intimacy with someone else and stay open. For some people this exercise is simple and no big issue. For others, this can be a huge deal. It all depends on your conditioning and the culture that you grew up in.

If this is a challenge for you, then repeat it daily for 21 days. You might even want to add in affirmations such as:

❖   'My body is beautiful.'

❖ 'My body is a part of nature.'

❖ 'My genitals are innocent and natural.'

Find out what helps you to open up and transform your relationship with your sexual organs. Bringing an attitude of curiosity and wonder, like a child, helps us to see innocence once again and thus return to our true nature.

What will you gain from these exercises?

The purpose of all of these exercises is twofold:

1. To heal shame, guilt and fear that we carry in the sexual organs and in our bodies.

2. To bring more consciousness to this area in the form of awareness, breath, light, smiling (love and acceptance) and attention.

Thus we replace shame patterns with pure awareness. In this way, even the most subtle and gentle of practices can really make deep shifts within us. This is a vital foundation for all other Tantric practices.

Why focus on sexuality?

Tantra is a holistic path: it is about all of life and works with our life-force energy, which is grounded in nature and our raw sexual energy, and so Tantra uses this energy as rocket fuel for our awakening.

The sexual centre (the genital area) sits at the base of our torso. When we sit in meditation, the genital area is grounded on the earth and is known in energetic terms as the 'root chakra' (*see page 106*). It is the base and root of the energetic system. Therefore, in order to activate life-force energy throughout our body and chakra system, we need to have an open and activated root chakra.

*If we are repressing our sexuality, we are
also suppressing the sexual energy.*

But we do not aim to stay at the root. Tantra is not about awakening sexuality and then just staying focused on sex! It is about awakening your sexuality and then discovering how to work with that potent energy to activate higher levels of energy, vibration and awareness.

Sexual healing

A few years into my first Tantric relationship (which lasted nine years in total), I started to feel pain in my pelvis. I went for a scan and was shocked to discover that I had a large ovarian cyst. The doctor told me that it needed to be surgically removed in three months' time, so I decided to use that time to find some alternative healing.

Armed with a copy of Women's Bodies, Women's Wisdom *by Dr Christiane Northrup, and my Taoist sexual practices, I decided to live in nature and spend time alone and in darkness to facilitate my own healing. I had read a book called* The Mysteries of the Dark Moon Goddess *by Demetra George, which was all about the development of a shadow and healing those suppressed aspects by entering the darkness and reclaiming them.*

*Living in a basic hut deep in the jungle, each night I
would get into my hammock and blow out my candle
and then face my fears in the darkness that surrounded
me. The undergrowth chirped and croaked and
whistled and howled, and strange creatures rustled by.
I even sighted a snake so long that it went on and on
and on as it slid past me, so I knew there were even
deadly creatures there.*

*I would do my Taoist sexual practices, breathing
into my ovaries and womb. I spent a lot of time just
bringing my conscious awareness to the energy in this
part of my body. At first this energy often appeared as
fear, but as I brought my breath and awareness to it, it
seemed to transform into pure energy and sometimes
even flowed up through me as an orgasmic wave.*

*Coupled with the fears that I felt from the nature around
me, step by step I faced fear with total consciousness
and watched the inner transformation happen.*

In essence I became alive again.

*Each piece of trapped fear seemed to rise up through
me as a stream of energy, bringing me to life.
Sometimes my body would shake with the amount of
energy that was awakening.*

*I thought often of the metaphors of snakes that are
used to describe the awakening of Tantric energies: the
kundalini serpent is depicted as a snake asleep at the
base of the spine, which can awaken and rise up the
spine activating the whole body. We are often so afraid
of snakes, just as we are taught to be afraid of our own*

sexual energy and power. But there is so much energy there, ready to awaken.

The other part of my journey was about reclaiming my creativity. As I breathed into my ovaries and other sexual organs, I began to become aware of my relationship to creativity. As a young child I found great joy in painting, singing and dancing. But as I grew up my culture taught me that these were unimportant and secondary to useful skills like maths and science. I dutifully put aside my creative endeavours in order to succeed in these apparently important areas.

By high school I was a physics scholar studying physics, biology, maths and economics! I had made it, but at the price of my creativity and my sexual health.

As I breathed into my sexual organs, I suddenly reconnected with the part of me that loved creativity, almost like a memory but stronger. It was like finding my little creative child hidden in a dark corner inside of me with her paintbrushes and songbooks in hand. Crouched as if being told off.

When I found her, I cried a river of tears. It felt as if I cried all night there in my hammock in the wild jungle. I sobbed my sadness at all of the years of blocked creativity. I cried my joy in re-finding this part.

The next morning I bent my knees, let out a howl of pain and gave birth to a river of blood. My period was not due, and I somehow knew that I was releasing the cyst. I did not need it any more.

When I returned to the hospital a few weeks later they were shocked at the mystery of where this huge cyst had gone.

From that day on, I embraced creativity like the air I breathed. I sang and danced every day. I ran an 'open mic' night. I explored sharing poetry, songs, dance of different genres. I studied belly dance and erotic dancing. I picked up the guitar and a 28-stringed autoharp. I studied some Indian classical songs. I played with comedy improvisation. There is no limit to my creativity (nor anyone else's), and the greatest source of joy in my life to this day comes from my creativity!

My intention in sharing my jungle experience is to show how:

- ❖ Suppressing creativity and blocking fears can result in us feeling, dead, dull and blocked.

- ❖ Energy comes from releasing suppressed fear in the presence of conscious awareness.

- ❖ The light of consciousness can unite with the darkness of the unconsciousness, and the resulting fusion brings a sense of awakening.

- ❖ Sexual energy and creative energy are one. Block sexuality and we affect our creativity.

- ❖ Physical illnesses may have a deeper energetic and psychological root.

- ❖ Nature has a healing effect.

- ❖ Returning from sexual conditioning to sexual nature brings a sense of liberation.

SUMMARY

* Before developing a Tantric sexuality, we often need to heal some old patterns and beliefs.

* It is important to bring healing and awareness to the root area of the body as it holds the potential of the life-force energy that can power up the rest of our body and our lives!

* The negative messages and lessons we received as children about sexuality often block the energy flow.

* It is not only about freeing the sexual energy but also channelling it (this makes Tantra different from the field of Conscious Sexuality).

* Sexual energy is closely connected to nature and our own naturalness.

* Sexual energy is our creative force.

Chapter 13

Awakening Sexual Energy

'Tantra acknowledges that sex is at the root of life and that to make human sexuality and erotic union a form of worship and meditation is to practise reverence for life.'

Margot Anand

After healing our conditioning about sexuality and our bodies in a gentle way, we can start to allow the sexual energy to awaken into a field of awareness. Of course, you may already feel that you have a lot of sexual energy alive within you, in which case focus more on being present with it. Or you may feel that it is still sleeping, in which case focus more on the practices to awaken it. Tantra awakens energy in a different way than society would generally activate it, so even if you feel sexually alive and liberated it is worth taking the steps to see what unfolds.

In Tantra, awakening sexual energy is not only about feeling sexier but about increasing our whole energetic experience of life, including:

- Activating our vitality and *joie de vivre*!

- Feeling sexual, without an overwhelming sexual horniness.

- Connecting us more deeply to the earth, nature and all of the energy that runs through nature.

- Activating our creative energy so that we start to feel a spontaneous creativity flowing through us.

In essence: awakening sexual energy
makes us feel MORE ALIVE!

There are three keys to awakening sexual energy, a process that is often termed 'awakening the snake' due to the way the energy uncoils and snakes up the spine. The three keys are:

1. Sound

2. Movement

3. Breath

These are very simple, yet we tend to have unconscious blocks that hold us back in all three areas. In order to be fully alive to sexual energy, we need to consider the body in a state of orgasm: the movement of energy creates a physical movement in the body; breathing gets deeper; and, unless suppressed, the breath then carries a sound.

Therefore, to awaken sexual energy we can deepen these three aspects and thus train the body to remember its natural state of full-body bliss.

In using these practices it is important to have a private space where you can make sounds without disturbing anyone. You want to free up your voice so don't want to feel hindered by being worried that you'll disturb the neighbours. Try to find a private space and, if necessary, play loud music to cover up your vocal sounds, if you think you might feel self-conscious.

With these practices it's also important to maintain a high level of internal awareness. In other words to stay authentic. If you are only focusing on making movements and sounds and strong breathing, you can start to develop a fake orgasmic nature rather than an authentic one. Thus the foundation for this series of practices is the following 'Shakti meditation', which helps us to drop in and be deeply present with the movements of energy within.

Practice: Shakti meditation

Practise the following meditation regularly – either as a solo or shared. It is an excellent foundation practice, as the meditation brings awareness and energy together and has healing effects as a result of this union. It is particularly powerful to use whenever you have an uncomfortable feeling or emotion going on. By bringing awareness to the sensations, energy can move where it has become blocked and facilitate the body's natural healing process.

Solo Shakti meditation

1. Lie down on the floor on a blanket or yoga mat. Do not have your head on a pillow as this can block the energy flow in your neck.

2. Make sure your arms and legs are uncrossed and relaxed, and take a few deep breaths to settle.

3. Now simply look inside your body and notice what is calling your attention. There is always some sort of sensation going on in the body, so just see which sensation calls your focus. You do not need to make something happen, just observe what is happening.

4. Now look at this sensation with an attitude of curiosity and innocence. Do not try to understand it, label it, diagnose it or judge it. The mind wants to jump right in there and analyse what it detects, but instead just choose an open-minded attitude and allow direct experiencing.

5. Increase the direct experiencing by describing the sensation out loud. For example:

    ❖   'I am noticing a tingling sensation at the base of my spine.'

    ❖   'Now I am noticing a warmth spreading outwards across my sacrum bone.'

    ❖   'I am noticing a pulse right at the tip of my tailbone.'

    The sensation could be anywhere in your body, and you might have sensations on the surface or deep inside the body. Describe them in detail, as if describing a flower to a blind person. The more detailed the description becomes the deeper you are penetrating your awareness into your energy.

6. Continue for about 10 minutes, observing and describing the most noticeable sensation at any one moment.

7. Sometimes the body might shake or shudder spontaneously during this meditation. If that happens, just allow it. It is simply when a lot of energy moves.

8. Rest in silence a few minutes more, and notice the effects of this meditation.

Shared Shakti meditation

This meditation can also be done in a pair or small group. In a pair you would lie side by side, and in a small group of up to six people you can lie with your heads all together at the centre and your bodies radiating outwards in all directions. Make sure that all of the bodies can lie fully outstretched, as it's important to be rested fully on the floor.

1. Take a few minutes to settle down by taking deep breaths.

2. Begin to scan inside and see what sensations catch your attention. Remember you do not have to try to make anything happen, just observe what is.

3. One by one you speak out what you are observing with the word 'I am noticing that...'

4. Make sure you do not label things such as, 'I am noticing fear/anger/ sadness' or judge them by saying, for example, 'I have a bad feeling in my belly.. Rather describe them neutrally, for example: 'I am noticing a tight clenching feeling in my belly.'

5. Listen to each other.

6. After 10 minutes you can rest in silence together a few minutes more before sitting up.

Tantric sounding

As mentioned, one of the three keys is sound. Sound is a form of energy, and we can release blocked energy a lot more easily when we can make sounds. Sounding is the term used to describe moving energy with the voice. It is not about singing or talking, but letting go of tension through a freely expressed sound.

The foundation of sounding is the humble sigh. Do not underestimate the power of a simple sigh! We think of sighing when we are tired or stressed, and indeed this is the body's way to let off steam. You get home from work, put your feet up and let out a long deep sigh: 'ahhhhh'. Immediately you feel better, and this is sounding.

Tantric sounding is a method to encourage energy to flow and help us let go of blocks, and also has the great advantage of being heard by others. When we hear someone's sound we actually receive a massive amount of information about where they are at in their lives. Our mind may not understand this information, but our body understands it deeply and often responds.

This is why it is helpful to sound during any form of intimacy with another person. It helps us to tune in to each other a lot more. Think about being stroked by a lover. If you stay silent they get no information about how you are receiving their touch. If you start to sigh and allow sounds, however, they immediately get feedback directly from your energy system to theirs.

Practice: Shakti sounding

1. Start Shakti meditation (*see page 145*) alone or with others.

2. At the end of the period of describing sensations, switch to expressing the sensations through sound. Start with a deep inhale and a sigh on the out-breath. Allow the sounds to express the sensations.

3. If you are in a pair or a group you can sound at the same time as each other, but listen to each other's sounds and also to the composite sound.

After 5 minutes of sounding, drop back into silence and rest.

Movement: Awakening the pelvis

The sexual energy lies coiled in the pelvis. To awaken it, it is essential to get the hips moving. If the hips are stiff and tight then the sexual energy will not be able to awaken and flow with ease. We may have stiff hips from sitting at a desk all day. However, our conditioning also affects this part of our body, and sexual shame tends to make us tighten up in this area.

Ways to awaken the pelvis:

❖ Dance like Elvis! Put on some good tunes and start trusting your hips to the beat. There is no coincidence that Elvis, James Brown and Tom Jones were renowned for their sexuality! If you want female inspiration, just look up a video of Beyoncé dancing!

❖ Take up a hip-focused dance form such as salsa or belly dance.

❖ Practise hip-opening positions from yoga.

❖ Learn qigong forms that work with the hips. Almost all qigong will have you sink down into your hips and open up the joints.

❖ Create your own hip practice each day, circling your hips and thrusting them. Find as many ways to move them as you can!

❖ For women there is a Taoist Sexual Art known as 'the jade egg practice'. This activates the whole vagina and creates deep healing. It is best to learn at first with a teacher. Once you are initiated, you can use your jade egg in your hip-opening practices. (Jade eggs and a DVD, *Tantric Jade Egg Practices*, are available on shashisolluna.com)

Tantric breath

To become more relaxed it is best to breathe through your nose. However, to activate your Tantric energy you want to breathe through an open mouth. You cannot orgasm with a closed mouth! When we are orgasmic our mouth automatically opens. We tend to hold a lot of tension from control in the jaw, and so practising open-mouthed Tantric Breathing helps us to let go of deep holding patterns of control.

Practice: Sexual energy awakening

Now we can put these principles and practices all together and use them to awaken the sexual energy. Take care not to push yourself, as this energy can be strong. It is best to be gentle and very conscious with each sensation, so you do not lose your awareness.

1. Start by putting on some uplifting energy that gets you going and have a dance around your room. Add a few hip thrusts in from time to time to really open the hips. You can also jump up and down a

few times which helps activate this whole area of the body.

2. After a few minutes of dancing lie down on a yoga mat or blanket and bend your knees with your feet flat on the floor.

3. Take 5 minutes of Shakti meditation (*see page 145*) to bring awareness inside your body.

4. Now start to move your hips around in any way that feels good. Exaggerate the movements, giving yourself lots of space and freedom to move. You can lift the hips up, circle them, twist them, bounce your hips fast on the floor, shake them and so on.

5. Breathe through an open mouth as you move. Take the breath all the way down to the hips.

6. Now add in your sounding, with long sighs on each exhale. As you feel sensations allow a free-form sounding, expressing whatever is alive within you.

7. Take 10 minutes to move, breathe and sound in this way.

8. Then rest on your back in silence, observing whatever is alive within you.

SUMMARY

♦ Awakening sexual energy is about activating our primal life-force energy: it awakens our creativity, vitality and aliveness.

♦ Sound, movement and breath are three keys to starting the awakening process.

♦ Movement of the hips is especially important.

❖ It is important to bring a lot of awareness to the process: Shiva (consciousness) must be there to hold Shakti (energy).

❖ Practise Shakti meditation to enhance connection between consciousness and energy, and safely awaken the energy body.

Chapter 14
Awakening Full-body Energy

*'Kundalini unfolding, the path to radical freedom,
is the soul's journey... It is a journey of absolute
transcendence while becoming fully alive and
present in your life now. It answers your deepest
yearnings for freedom, purpose, meaning, and love.'*

LAWRENCE EDWARDS

Once your sexual energy is alive and activated, then you'll want to awaken all of your body's energy centres, or 'chakras' (*see page 106*). This is so that the energy can rise upwards through the whole body, taking us into full-body bliss and sublimation. It also has healing effects on many different areas of our life, as each chakra affects different levels of our reality.

Hence in this chapter you'll discover the practices that pave the way for full-body orgasm and higher states of consciousness.

Activating the energy channels

Tantra is about full-body awakening, not just a shift of the mind or consciousness. This awakening is known as the awakening of the 'energy body'. The energy body is the life force that flows through and around the physical body.

When the full body is awakened then a person has an aliveness and radiance about them.

Classical Tantric theory says that it is through the activation of the energy body that the mind can awaken to its true nature: we activate Shakti energy to awaken Shiva consciousness. In fact some definitions of classical Tantra state that Tantra is the path of worshipping the Divine Feminine.

This does not mean it is about simply worshipping a goddess statue, but that honouring the divinity in the energetic flow of life, we also meet the source of that energy. In other words, the path to God is the Goddess. The path to Truth is through Love. The Tantric path to awakening is via energy activation. Shiva says,

'I am everywhere, infusing everything.
To find me,
Become absorbed in intense experience.
Go all the way.
Be drenched in the energies of life.
Enter the world beyond separation.
The light of a candle reveals a room.
The rays of the sun reveal the world.
So does the Divine Feminine
Illumine the way to Me.'

Excerpted from *The Radiance Sutras* © 2014 Lorin Roche with permission from Sounds True, inc.

As described in Chapter 9 (*see page 95*) one of the highest principles and aims of Tantra is to see the Divine in and through everything. Think about people or things that are full of life-force energy compared to those with little or none. For example, if you took a plastic umbrella and a living pot plant and pondered which one you could feel God through, most people would choose the plant. Or the choice between walking in a concrete city or hiking in nature – most people would feel the presence of Spirit in the nature setting. This is due to the flow of life-force energy.

It is through this mysterious phenomenon called Shakti that we can find the Divine in everyday life.

Sometimes you may meet a person overflowing with life-force energy. They appear so alive and so radiant, you might say that they have 'spirit' or are a spirited person. Some great performers can move so much energy when they sing or dance that people have a transcendental experience just watching them! It is no wonder that people virtually worship great performers!

Tantra recognizes that Shakti is the purest embodiment of Shiva; this life-force energy is the pure embodiment of the Highest Consciousness. Thus a Tantric practitioner aims to awaken their energy within so that they can become aligned with their highest nature within this life. It is not just about feeling alive and looking radiant, but about the creative energy that powers up your life. When this current of life force is flowing through you and your life, you will feel that you are truly living your life purpose.

Tantra 101

As described earlier, the most revered stream of life-force energy is called 'kundalini' and is compared to a snake rising. Once a person's kundalini is activated, they are powered up by this divine energy in their life, and this serpent rising metaphor is describing the sublimation of sexual energy (*see page 89*).

If we suppress or leak our sexual energy then we keep it trapped at the base of the spine in its sleep mode. If we reject our sexual power, then we release our sexual energy downwards towards the earth rather than up into the body towards the heavens. However, through Tantric practice and healing we can learn to raise the energy upwards, allowing the Shakti to rise and, ultimately, the kundalini to awaken. This is the full-body aliveness and awakening that Tantra aims for.

What does it mean to 'raise energy'?

Raising energy can sound like some far-off new-age concept, but actually it is something that we all know. Either you have experienced it, or at least seen it in great performers or dancers.

Raising energy is when we lift our energy higher than our everyday normative level. For example, you may go to a nightclub and dance until you feel elated and liberated. Or possibly you love salsa clubs or some sort of dance style that lifts your spirits. Some people raise energy through singing, especially ecstatic songs such as gospel or elevated music such as religious music or kirtan (devotional singing that is popular in the yoga scene). Other people take up hobbies such as skydiving or rock climbing, which elevate their energy levels.

All of these are ways to raise energy and we all have an in-built desire for that. Why? Because it lifts us up out of the everyday humdrum reality. Without raising energy we can easily become stuck in routines and patterns, and sometimes even feel trapped by our own lives.

However, many people let this desire for raising energy become unconscious. They seek ways of getting high using drugs or alcohol. This creates a temporary release from the stagnant feeling of everyday life, but if it is done unconsciously then it creates a separation between the high and the low. People then experience the comedown feeling when they are not high any more. It's easy to form addictions, as people become desperate to get high again. And because the high is not rooted in everyday reality, people then feel torn between two selves, and sometimes there is a fight or struggle between the two. This causes a lot of pain and suffering.

Tantric energetics is about consciously raising energy, from the heavier energies up to the higher lighter vibrations. It is like playing musical notes from the deep bass notes all the way up to the high notes. It's not about getting away from the heavier more grounded parts of our lives, but about including expanded moments when we feel high and open, and being able to move between the two gracefully. These expanded moments might be through Tantric lovemaking, but also through dance, song, creativity, yoga, breathwork and energy work.

This way we feel that we are expressing the full range of life-force energy in our lives. We feel full and total. High and yet grounded. It is like a musical instrument that only plays the bottom two or three bass notes. The music will sound fuller and more complete if you include the whole octave of notes.

Our lives feel more complete when
we raise energy; when we feel and
express energies in the full range.

As we raise energy, we feel more open and alive. Any blocks where energy was not flowing will become opened up as we activate energy. Energy blocks manifest as feeling stuck, shut down and shielded. They can also manifest into emotional and physical distortions and illnesses, whereas free-flowing energy helps us feel radiantly alive and well. Energy rising up is like water rushing through pipes, clearing away any dirt that has gathered there and bringing a fresh new feel to everything.

If we combine meditation with raising energy, then we unite the Shiva and Shakti principles. It is not just about becoming high now and again. If we can stay deeply conscious as we raise energy, then we start to cultivate very profound states of meditation and very high states of consciousness.

Exercise: How is your energy?

Read through the following questions to contemplate how energy moves within you, and where it might get stuck.

❖ **Flow:** Do you feel stuck in life? Do you feel bogged down by routines and the daily grind? If so, you may not be raising energy in your life.

❖ **Movement:** What activities lift you up? Make a list of things that uplift you. Then check in how often you do them.

❖ **Resistances and blocks:** What kinds of excuses do you give to yourself to avoid doing the activities listed above? Are you too busy doing other things? Too lazy? Too tired?

❖ **Consciousness:** How many activities that raise energy do you think you do unconsciously? Do you use drugs or alcohol, or other ways that mean you lose consciousness when you get high? What ways do your raise energy and remain conscious and present?

❖ **Groundedness:** Do you find that you can raise energy and yet stay grounded, or do you lose yourself/ lose contact with everyday activities in favour of feeling high?

❖ **Creativity:** When energy flows, so does creativity. How creative do you feel yourself to be? What are your creative expressions and forms? Do you find it easy to improvise? Do you find it easy to express yourself? Do you find it easy to be spontaneous?

❖ **Sensitivity:** How sensitive are you to energy? Do you feel energy in people? In a room? Can you feel someone without touching them?

These contemplations should give you an idea of how energy flows within you. Try to get an idea of how it is within you without making any judgement. Simply observe with an attitude of interest and deeper understanding. It is not about judging the way you are as good or bad, but simply gaining more awareness.

As you start some Tantric practices, return to these questions from time to time to see how your energy body is shifting.

Awakening energy through nature

So how can we awaken our energy body? The classic model used is known as the 'chakra system', as described in Chapter 10 (*see page 106*). Chakra means a wheel, and it is like the water wheels that pump energy flow through the body. If one wheel is a bit stiff or slow, then it affects the flow throughout the whole system. The chakras can be activated in many different ways.

In the ancient systems of Tantra the elements of nature associated with each chakra could be used to awaken the energy within it. When we immerse ourselves in nature we can let the energy there support our return to our own true nature. Nature is understood to be the ultimate source of life-force energy, or *Para-Shakti*.

Shakti is also known as the feminine principle and the goddess. This is not so unusual: many cultures have equated nature with the Divine Feminine. Mother Nature is a common phrase and in South America she is called *Pachamama*. In Tao the earth is known as the source of the yin, or feminine energy (*see page 102*). So the fact that Tantra sees nature as the source of life-force energy is quite aligned with other traditions. The presence that we take into nature is our 'Shiva' or masculine aspect. When we are present in nature, Shiva and Shakti unite, facilitating our awakening.

Though nature is the one great Shakti, there are many different forms of nature's energies. Each one is called a different Shakti. For example, we find earth Shakti in the ground and we find water Shakti in a lake. Each natural energy can help to heal and awaken the energy within us to restore our energy body to its natural and alive state.

We can also use each element to understand that energy in our life. For example earth energy is not only about the soil and mud, but also about the grounding in our own lives: the amount of stability and structure we have in life, and how deep our family bonding is (our roots). It is important to work on each chakra so that we have a clear channel running through us. It is a hindrance to raise energy when we have blockages along the way.

The five elements

Tantra works with the energy of the five elements of nature. These correspond to the first five chakras (*see page 106*). In classical Tantra, these elements are:

1. Earth

2. Water

3. Fire

4. Air

5. Ether

To awaken our own energy system we can connect to each of these energies. They are generally activated in order from earth to ether. This is because of the flow of energy through the system. This activation has the effect of healing and purifying our energy, and thus our sexuality, our emotions and our wellbeing.

Earth

This element is associated with the root chakra (muladhara) at the base of the spine (*see page 106*). It is the energy of the earth, soil, mud and rocks: solid, earthy energy. There is a phrase used in Tantra that says, 'No mud, no lotus'. This means that without access to the earth primal energy of the root chakra, we cannot activate the heavenly sublime energy at the crown (symbolized by the lotus).

In the human body, the earth Shakti is our primal life-force energy. It is the basest form of sexual energy in that this energy just wants to have sex! In some cultures they even call this kind of sex 'having a root'. If we do not lift energy above this level, we will always stay like an animal in our sexuality... sex for the sake of reproduction or base desire. However, we need to activate this level of sexuality before we can go higher.

Earth can be grounding and stabilizing. But too much earth can make us feel stuck and blocked.

❖ How is the stability in your life? Do you have a stable home/job/life? Or are you lacking foundation?

❖ Do you have so much stability that you feel stuck, as if stuck in the mud? Or do you have so little stability that you feel unstable?

❖ How is the earth element in your life? What is your connection to the earth, the soil, the rocks and the mud? Do you ever get your feet muddy or sink your toes into the fresh grass?

❖ How do you feel about being in a physical body? Are you comfortable with your animal nature?

❖ How is your connection to your ancestors: your family, your home, your 'roots'?

Walking barefoot on the earth can activate the earth Shakti, taking a mud bath or mud wrap, getting your hands muddy and working with the earth. (*For more on working with the elements, see page 167*).

Water

This element is associated with the second chakra (svadhisthana) located above the pubic bone at the level of the genitals (*see page 106*). It is thus associated with sexuality. It is the energy of the vast ocean, gushing waterfalls, bubbling brooks and still, deep lakes. Water flows into all crevices and nourishes what has become dry and withered. Without sexual energy in our lives, we too can become dry and withered.

Water is deep and mysterious. It is often used symbolically to represent the unconscious realm, and sexuality is often merged with unconsciousness or drugs and alcohol if we are not careful. Water is also the emotional realm. We can be under-emotional, overemotional or naturally emotional.

❖ Water can stagnate and become like a murky swamp or purified and become like a pristine lake. How is the flow of energy in your life? Does everything flow along gracefully?

❖ Are you drowning in heavy emotions?

❖ Are you drawn to unconsciousness or losing consciousness, such as with alcohol and drugs?

❖ How is your sexuality – is it conscious and healthy or something you repress or distort?

- Are you too soft and fluid that everyone can push you around?

- Do you feel easily emotionally affected by events around you? Or do you feel that you have a cool and clear depth about you?

Bathing rituals such as going to a spa and bathing in natural waters or springs can activate the element. (*For more on working with the elements, see page 167*).

Fire

The fire element is associated with the third chakra (manipura) located above the navel (*see page 106*). Fire is an uprising energy. It is passionate and hot. It is desire. It burns away the old and creates an alchemy for transformation. It can also destroy and burn.

In its distortion, fire is aggression and violence. In its purification it is pure energy and passion. In distortion, fire is egoic desire. In purification it is divine desire.

Fire is an energy so powerful that many of us are afraid of it. But if we hold back our fire, we may also hold back our passion. We may block our empowerment.

- How is your relationship to power?

- Do you consider yourself a powerful person? Is your power about having power over others or is it the power of love?

- Do you feel uplifting energy in your body?

✦ Do you often feel like dancing or making love with passion? How are you with natural fire – do you like to play with fire or exercise extra caution with it?

✦ Are you drawn to the sunshine and warmth?

✦ Are you a warm person?

Fire can be tricky to work with. It is important to purify the ego tendencies, so that we do not misuse power or build more ego. One of the best remedies for this in Tantra is Bhakti or devotion. Directing our passions towards worshipping the Divine is a potent way to purify our inner fire.

Air

This element is associated with the fourth chakra (anahata) located at the centre of the chest (*see page 106*). This is the heart chakra. Air is light, subtle, expanding. When we are elated we dance on air. Think of fairies and angels or beings of light dancing in the air.

Air is the breath, which expands our lungs and makes more room for love in our hearts; it can be uplifting but also chaotic and uncontained. It can make us feel light, but too much air can make us feel pushed around. Air can open our lungs, but it can also choke us, as in the grief of a broken heart.

The air caresses our skin like a tender lover. It whispers secrets in our ear.

✦ Are you a light person? Do you feel light-hearted? Or do you sigh all of the time with a heavy heart?

+ Do you ever feel like you are dancing on air?

+ Is your breathing smooth and steady or jarred and irregular?

+ Do you feel the sweet breeze of love's essence in the space around you?

+ Do you feel a force of chaos in your life?

+ Are you blown around by life's wind?

Connect to the air by walking along windy clifftops or standing in a breeze. Dance on your tiptoes. Blow a dandelion. Fly a kite. Skip along through a field of flowers. Practice pranayama or Tantric breathing meditations (*see page 33*).

Ether

The ether element is space. It is about the etheric realm, beyond this tangible world. The ether leads us into timelessness.

It is associated with the fifth chakra (vishuddha) located at the throat (*see page 107*). Its activation can take us beyond our controlled behaviour and into pure creativity and spontaneity (*see page 144*). There is a state in which creativity pours through us with no planning – this is the ether, Divine Creativity. Sometimes two or more people tune in together and begin a shared creativity, and it is transpersonal.

Ether takes us into the Beyond. It can take us to deep meditation or make us feel spacey. Some people even get 'lost in space'.

The Ether can reveal to us the Tandava – Shiva's dance (*see page 44*). This is the divine unfolding... when movements or words or creativity seem to come straight from God. This is sometimes called 'channelling'.

When we lift into the realm of Ether, we are with the stars. We are expanding into space. Time stops and extends at the same time. Floating on clouds of bliss, you have entered the etheric realm.

❖ Do you ever contemplate space?

❖ Are you tied to time and deadlines or do you know how to access timelessness?

❖ Have you ever experienced being a creative channel: speaking words or singing songs that just come through you?

❖ Are you comfortable to improvise?

❖ How much spontaneity is there in your life?

❖ Do you ever expand into states of bliss? What takes you there?

Enter the ether by lying on your back looking at the stars. Look between the stars and contemplate empty space. Stare into a blue cloudless sky. Stand and imagine your body is dissolving into space.

How to work with the elements

Working with the elements of nature is a foundational aspect of Tantra. Kashmir Shaivism Tantra has a method known as the *Tattvas*, which is a metaphysical understanding of the nature of the universe all the way from the most tangible earth to the highest intangible heavens, pure consciousness. The five elements are in fact the first five Tattvas.

According to this theory, the way to awaken to highest consciousness is like rolling back the red carpet of life, all the way to Source. Thus we enter each element, then each sense and different aspects of consciousness and, through these practices, eventually we reach God/the Creator/Source and awaken to our divine nature.

A simplified version of the Tattvas is awakening the chakras. In Tantra this involves activating each elemental energy within yourself, starting with the earth and working upwards. This can be done in various ways, including:

✦ Yoga asana (postures) for each chakra.

✦ Meditation for each chakra.

✦ Special toning in each chakra or the recitation of mantra to activate each one.

✦ Meditating on '*yantras*' (*see page 179*).

✦ Dancing the energy of each chakra.

✦ Making love with the energy of each chakra.

These practices can all activate strong energies and so are best done under the guidance of a Tantra teacher. However, you can also begin to work on each chakra by working with nature itself and by imbibing the qualities into yourself. Here are some inspirations to activate each element:

Earth element

Go and work with the ground, growing vegetables. Get your hands muddy. Smell the earth as your work with it. Lie down on the earth and let yourself feel heavy. Sink your feet into mud until it squishes up between your toes. Let yourself get soil on your skin and surrender to getting muddy. Dance like an African dancer. Stomp your feet on the floor.

Water element

Swim, swim, swim in the ocean, in lakes, in the river. Float in the water and let its current carry you. Wash yourself in a waterfall or float in the bathtub for an hour until you become one with the water. Drink water with awareness as it flows down your throat. Dance in fluid ways, as if you are dancing underwater.

Fire element

Lie in the sun and enjoy the warmth on your skin. Sit by a roaring log fire, watching the flames. Walk on hot coals or do a sweat lodge or sauna ritual (with guidance!). You don't need a long time with the fire element; just be total with it whilst it is there. Take up salsa, tango or flamenco.

Air element

Stand in the breeze and meditate upon it as it touches your skin, feel it caressing you. Breathe and let your breath merge with the air around you. Watch the leaves being danced around in a strong wind. Fly a kite. Dance on your tiptoes or take up Sufi whirling as if being whirled on the wind.

Ether element

Lie under a starry sky and look into the vast universe. Hide away your watch and turn off your phone and let yourself get lost in some vast landscape for a timeless amount of time. Go to grand landscapes in which you feel very small, such as mountaintops and canyons. Feel all that is greater than you and dissolve into that. Try contact dance or improvisational dance, so that you can move beyond form.

The higher chakras

You may have noticed that there are five elements but seven chakras (*see page 106*). It is as if the five elements are a stepladder to raise energy upwards to the higher chakras.

As energy flows upwards through the body, a very powerful state of meditation is attained, which makes it possible for the third eye to open – the sixth chakra (ajna). As a result, the practitioner experiences a powerful shift in perception and sees the source of all of life – seeing love at the heart of everything, or seeing God everywhere.

As the energy continues to builds through the sixth chakra, the seventh chakra (sahasrara) opens. In this the practitioner experiences a full union with God or all of existence. It is stronger even than a shift in perception. Some Tantrics describe it as 'making love with God'. Osho described this as '*mahamudra*', a term taken from Tibetan Buddhism that can be translated as 'the great gesture'.

Tantra 101

There was an ancient ritual practiced in Tantra called '*Maituna*' that activated each chakra through ritual, special food and drinks and lovemaking. This was a method used to attain such a union with Existence. It was known to be very powerful. However, it was also judged by many spiritual groups in India at the time as being morally questionable because of its use of meat, fish, alcohol and sex.

Once all of the chakras are activated and alive with energy, then the inner pathway from the earth to the heavens is opened. Sometimes this is called the 'inner flute'. The practitioner then gets to experience an embodied enlightenment: the experience of being both divine and in a physical body.

Lovemaking to God

When I was studying at a Tantra school I experienced a lovemaking experience that would change my life. I got together with a man who really knew what he was doing! As we made love, he guided me to breathe into different parts of my body and put attention there. He worked chakra by chakra and directed the energy to each place as he made love.

It was quite astounding how I could feel energy building at each centre. I'm not sure if I could even call it pleasure or pain, it was just intense! It would build and build until eventually something would feel as if it cracked through and it would rise up to the next area. Sometimes I would express emotions or sounds and he skilfully guided me into my breath to stay with the energy and not discharge it all cathartically.

Gradually the energy rose all the way to my throat, rising up with force and pressure through this narrowing in my body, and then BOOM! It cracked right into my third eye, like a bolt of lightning! And my eyes were flung open from within, and I saw him God-like before me, his skin shimmering with gold. I saw not his personality, but God in human form. And even more remarkable, I felt my own divinity radiating through me and shining out of my face like a beam of light.

The lovemaking became a meeting of God and Goddess. My veils fell away, my masks, my defences all gone. Radiance and light were replacing the physical form. I was a shimmering body of light, made of waves of vibration that met and merged with the light waves of his being. After some timeless time merging, we moved into meditation and I was simply in a full state of bliss: reunited with the light of the universe – like a ray of light dissolving back into the sun. Fullness. Emptiness. One with all that is. Pure Love. Home.

Practice: Five-element massage

One of the most powerful ways to activate energy is through conscious touch. Tantric lovers are not just trying to turn each other on, but to awaken energy in their partner, and massage has the advantage of giving lovers a wider range of styles of touching and connecting.

It can be even more powerful to play music during the massage, so for each element I will make suggestions of the types of music you could play (*see page 173*).

Preparation

❖   Create a sacred space together. It could be on a double bed or a
    mattress on the floor. Make sure you have an undisturbed time.
    Create atmosphere with softer lighting, candles, incense and
    whatever feels good to you (*see page 52*).

❖   This is best done with clothes on as it is about touch rather than
    massage, but it feels good to be naked under a sarong or wear
    loose clothing.

❖   For each element, offer touch for 5–10 minutes. At the end hold your
    hands still on your partner's belly or lower back for 20 seconds and
    then slowly lift them off.

❖   One partner gives and the other receives and later on you can
    exchange.

❖   The receiving partner can lie on their belly or on their back for the
    whole session, as they prefer.

Technique

Earth: The earth touch is a solid, unmoving pressure. You can place hands
on your partner's body and then gradually lean in using your body weight.
Rest in the position for about 30 seconds before slowly lifting off. Never
lean on top of a joint in the body, and feel into your partner to make sure
they are relaxed to your touch. If they tense up, then lighten your touch.
You can also transmit earth touch by lying on top of your partner's body
and just resting there. Lower down and up with care so that you do not hurt
them. Try to imbibe earthiness whilst you touch.

Suggested music: Deep didgeridoo

Water: The water touch is about flow. So with a gentle pressure let your
hands flow all over their body in continuous motion like a stream. You
can add a little sensual quality, as the water activates the second chakra,

which is sensuous. Imagine you are guiding oil or fluids all over their body. Try to imbue the essence of water in your movements.

Suggested music: Flowing and sensual

Fire: The fire is about moving energy and it has a fun playful quality to the touch. You can rub their body, as if making it warm. Also light slaps. Rocking the body. Get the energy warmed up and moving!

Suggested music: Passionate, possibly Latin style

Air: This is the lightest, feather-light, physical touch with fingertips or very light hands. As this is associated with the heart chakra, you can also rest a hand on the front or the back of the heart. Caress with light delicacy. Stroke the face with tender fingertips. Let your touch be like a breeze upon their skin.

Suggested music: Light and airy, possibly hung drum music or flute music.

Ether: This is a non-physical touch. For this element you will caress their aura or energy body. Raise your hands above their head and stroke down towards the feet, a few inches away from the skin. You have a natural instinct of where the person's energy field is, so trust that. Always stroke from head to feet and not in the other direction, as this is very relaxing. This is also very subtle, so be very still and present as you give this caress.

Suggested music: Tibetan or crystal bowls

Completion: Leave your partner for 5–10 minutes to integrate this gift. Be very still as you sit beside them, as they are in a very subtle state. When you are ready to bring them back, touch the hand closest to you and whisper gently in their ear, 'You can open your eyes when you are ready, beloved.'

You may have noticed by now that one or two elements are stronger in you than others. Some people may be well balanced, but most of us will be naturally stronger in one or two of the elements, and the others we may have to work to activate. On one hand we resonate with places and people with a similar energy to us, but we also tend to become attracted to the energies we have yet to activate. This explains why a light fairy-like woman may hang out with other fairy-like women, yet be attracted to that earthy man who works with his hands in the forest all day.

To become a well-balanced Tantric lover, it is worth exploring your lovemaking elements and perhaps playing with those you are not so strong in. You can activate an element's energy by playing it out.

Another way to activate energy is known as 'transmission'. This is when someone awakens the energy in you. For example, if you wanted to receive a transmission to become a fierier, more passionate lover, you'd be wise to go and dance at a salsa club and imbibe that energy until you can express it yourself. Or if you happened to fall in love with a fiery passionate person, then you would receive transmission through your lovemaking and energy exchange.

Exercise: What kind of lover are you?

Read through the following descriptions to help determine what kind of lover you are and, if you have one, your partner is too. The guide is not intended to judge others or ourselves, but to understand energy even more deeply, so use it with care. For your growth, think of expanding into new areas rather than fixing a problem. The sexual arts are art forms. It is not about working out how to make love (we all have an in-built instinct for that); it is about expanding our repertoire!

Earthy lover

This lover likes rhythm: lovemaking is all about the body and penetration, the root element. Sometimes an earthy lover can even move the bed across the floor! Earthy lovers are often attracted to buttocks, or they may have strong buttocks and thighs themselves. Earthy lovers may like to make love in a primal animalistic kind of way, possibly taking their lover from behind.

Watery lover

This lover likes it erotic and sensual: they may like to bring exotic fruit or chocolate spread into their love play. They care about the setting, the atmosphere and the music, and like it to feel sexy! They care about sexy clothing and master the art of seduction. Watery lovers can be outrageous flirts, or simply exude such sensuality that people fall at their feet. They like touch, preferably with a lot of oil. It's all about the foreplay. This is the lovemaking with groans of pleasure and moans of delight.

Fiery lover

This lover likes to play with power and passion: they may pin you up against a wall or throw you onto the bed. They may pull your hair or play bite your skin. They like to go wild and let the energy take them over. There may be power play: one partner on top then they roll over and the other one is on top. If the earthy lover is the bull, the fiery lover is the tiger! This lover lets passion run the game and passions run wild in this exchange!

Airy lover

This is the lover of the heart: subtle with great sensitivity. This is not the place of the animal; it is the exchange of the tender lovers. This lover caresses your face as if you are the most precious being on earth. This lover looks deep into your eyes as they make love. It is not so much about the penetration as it is about the connection. You can feel your breath and your lover's breath merging together. It is lovemaking love.

Ether lover

This lover is from another planet! In their presence you feel as if transported to another realm. You get lost in their eternal eyes. This lover is all about the subtle. It is no longer about the touch but about the energy. Wave upon wave of energy shimmers through you as you make love. Two bodies merge into one in the great ocean of energy. This lovemaking is timeless. You experience subtle feelings that you could not even describe; you enter altered states. The whole lovemaking becomes a meditation.

Master lover

The master lover has learned to activate and share all of the energies and expressions in their lovemaking. They can take their partner on a journey from the earth to the heavens. They can be spontaneous and alive to any energy within their partner, responding to anything as it arises and meeting their beloved there. They know how to dance with any energy and they also know how to guide it masterfully into higher and higher realms to take their beloved into timeless bliss.

Awakening energy through divine inspiration

Nature and the elements is one way to awaken energy. In many paths of classical Tantra, the practitioner also uses divine vibrations and inspiration. This aspect of classical Tantra is often very hard for Westerners to grasp, as they often misunderstand it as worshipping a statue. Rather, it is like using vibrations that are closer to the Divine Truth than the vibes that are around us in everyday life.

Life is made up of vibration. Energy is constantly vibrating. In Tantra this shimmering movement is called '*spanda*'.

> *All Shakti, all life force is vibrating*
> *with life. The more alive we become,*
> *the more vibrant we become.*

When life energy is cut off from Source then it becomes distorted, which we call 'negative vibrations'. Or it may become so weak that it slows down, which we call a 'low vibration'. Some surroundings are full of low vibrations and negative vibrations and it is harder to remember your true divine nature in such surroundings.

A deity is a vibration close to or the same as the divine reality. It is representation of divine perfection, whether represented as a form (a statue), a geometrical shape (a yantra) or a sound (a mantra). Using deities is like having an archetype to aspire to. Maybe your parents weren't perfect role models, but you could contemplate statues of Shiva and Parvati as representations of the perfect role models. Who would you be, if they had been your parents? What would your childhood have been like? How can you be more like Shiva the God or Shakti the Goddess?

Tantra 101

Yantra and mantra are both terms found in classical Tantra and used to describe vibrations and tools to access certain frequencies of Shatki, or energy.

Yantra: A geometrical shape that one can meditate on by looking at it, often without blinking for many minutes at a time (*see below*). In fact it is said that by meditating on a yantra, once can activate certain energies within. There are yantras for different deities and different elements.

Mantra: This is the audio version of the visual yantra. A mantra is a sound that is chanted to activate energy and shift consciousness. When one is experienced with meditation, a mantra is often chanted silently. Of course, they may be used together, a specific geometrical shape with a specific chant.

A Tantric yantra (sri yantra)

In classical Tantra, every kind of energy in the universe has an ideal or perfected version of its form. Thus we have a goddess of beauty (Tripura Sundari) and a goddess of creativity (Sarasvati) and so on, which are representations of the ideal vibration of these qualities. By meditating with them in various ways, we can start to tune in our own personal frequency to the divine frequency. It is a method to help us to embody divine qualities.

In Tantra there are 10 goddesses known as the *Mahavidyas* (meaning 'great manifestation') who are frequently used as teaching tools for purifying and uplifting our energy. These are traditionally passed on with initiations so it is best to find a teacher or school that offers this (*see page 241*). They will usually give an energy initiation (*shaktipat*) followed by teaching how to use the mantras, yantras and meditations associated with that deity.

The many deities are not a replacement for the one great Truth. It is not about worshipping many gods. They are there as teachers and role models; bridges between the human and the Divine, in the same way that Christ is a human bridge to God in Christianity. They are potential vibrations that may lie dormant with you, that can be reawakened through intention and practice.

Tantra 101

Working with deities is not for everyone but it is a prominent part of classical Tantra, so it is worth being at least aware of it.

One method is to use deities for transfiguration – seeing those divine qualities in another. Rather than focusing on all of the bits of ourselves that we want to fix, we resonate with more of the divine qualities that we aspire to, and the lower qualities simply fall away.

SUMMARY

+ Make a commitment to listen to your heart.

+ Awakening full-body energy is a core aspect of the Tantric path. This means to awaken the energy at the root and let it flow up through all the energy centres (chakras).

+ There are specific channels that energy flows through, like streams.

+ Awakening energy is paralleled to an honouring of the feminine in life, as energy or 'Shakti' is seen as the divine feminine in ALL of us (yes, even in a man's body!).

+ Energy awakens and flows is response to our perceiving it, our honouring of it and even our devotion to it.

+ Pure life-force energy is seen as the perfect manifestation of God... it is thus the Goddess: God's perfect form. Thus tantrics seek to embody energy.

+ When we raise energy we lift our consciousness up above normal everyday levels.

+ Nature is a very pure manifestation of energy, and thus we can use nature to help us awaken and purify our own energy.

❖ There are different elements in nature and these are also seen within our chakras: earth, water, fire, air and ether are the classical five elements of the first five chakras.

❖ As you understand yourself and your sexuality through the chakras, you can see where to open up more to become more whole and complete in terms of energy.

❖ In classical tantra, the practitioner uses geometric shapes (yantras) and specific sounds (called mantras) to awaken energies. They may also work with deities to help them attain the highest level of that energy within themselves.

Chapter 15
The Art of Tantric Orgasm

'Truly, at the peak of orgasm, we pierce through the illusion of fragmentation and separation, and glimpse the unity and interconnectedness of all beings.'

Margot Anand

Possibly the most well-known aspect of Tantra is that of the full-body orgasm. If there is ever a reference to Tantra in movies, it is usually something relating to sex that goes on for hours and hours... Indeed, Tantra works with energy in a way in which the powerful life-force energy of orgasm can rise up throughout the whole body and take you into an altered state in which you feel a connection to all that is.

However, it is essential to take the preparatory steps first. These have already been covered in this book and they are:

1. Opening the heart (*see page 113*)

2. Purification and healing (*see page 123*)

3. Opening the energy centres and channels (*see page 153*)

As I mentioned in an earlier chapter, pushing our energy too fast can leave us feeling overwhelmed at best and traumatized at worst. A good friend of mine who teaches Tantra has a catchphrase, 'Tantra not Trauma'.

Opening the heart

This is a vital step in the process, and a good place to begin. Many systems of energy work recognize the heart as a bridge between the earth of the body and the sky of the spirit. In order for energy to flow from sex to spirit, we need the bridge of the heart to be open and ready. Love is the essential key that allows opposites to meet and unite.

Sex and spirit meet through the
heart, and love is the catalyst.

Purification and healing

Working with the shadow is important before raising strong energy. Sexual energy is massively creative and will multiply anything that exists. If you have a lot of guilt, fear, shame or distorted energy and emotions, then these could even get stronger if you throw fuel on the fire. Remember that traditional Tantric practitioners spend many years meditating and preparing before learning the sexual practices.

Take time to work on healing the big stuff before jumping to the strong energy work. Of course you don't have to wait until you are feeling 'perfect', just make sure you have spent time with some investigation and healing before moving on to energy practices.

Opening the energy centres and channels

You cannot run a current between earth and heaven without opening the energy channels. Orgasm is a current of energy, sexual energy, and it is carried through pathways. The Taoists called them 'meridians' and the Tantrics called them '*nadis*'.

Both systems are recognized energy hubs. Taoists had different names for each energy hub, and the Tantrics recognized them as the chakras (*see page 106*). Whichever system you use, opening the channels through yoga, qigong, stretching or breathing are all ideal practices to prepare for moving energy through the body with ease. Working with the elements (*see page 167*) also helps to activate each energy centre.

Once the foundations have been laid then you can begin a series of practices to develop an open energy body to facilitate full-body orgasm. The purpose of developing this is not to become a great lover so that you can show off to your mates, as such an intention would only nourish the ego. The purposes to develop full-body orgasm include:

1. **To open up to life energy and creative energy and allow it to flow through all parts of your body and your life.** Sexual energy is creative energy. We came here to offer our creative gifts to this life. We cannot do that if we are stopping that energy from flowing into its full capacity. Developing full-body orgasm is about opening up to our full creative potential.

2. **To heal the shadow and wounded parts of our life by uplifting them and raising their vibration.** Sublimation

has the healing effect of raising heavy energies and stubborn patterns, allowing them to transform in a deep inner alchemy. Full-body orgasm is a powerful self-healing mechanism.

3. **To align sex, love and spirit into wholeness.** We all long for integration, to feel whole and complete. Full-body orgasm unites sex, love and spirit, bringing us into a fulfilling place of totality.

4. **To use the powerful sexual energy as rocket-fuel for higher states of consciousness.** Sometimes people experience a feeling akin to prayer or total remembrance of the Divine Truth when they enter full-body orgasm.

5. **To extend the duration of orgasm in order that we might stay conscious within it.** Tantrics see orgasm as a profound state of consciousness. If it lasts only a couple of seconds, we cannot really enter it with our awareness. So learning full-body orgasm is about cultivating a powerful medium for meditation.

6. **To practise the art of dying.** So this may not be high on your agenda, but in spirituality learning to let go and surrender to a life force and consciousness that is greater than us is part of the spiritual progress. As Leonardo da Vinci once said: 'While I thought that I was learning how to live, I have been learning how to die.' Every time we surrender to full-body orgasm, we are learning how to die. The ego-self dies in the moment of orgasm – we simply cannot hold on to our pretences and masks at such a moment. Instead we learn to die to a greater truth and a reality that transcends even the passing experience of our own life.

In Lorin Roche's beautiful interpretation of the *Vigyan Bhairav, The Radiance Sutras* he writes:

> *'At the moment of orgasm the truth is illumined,*
> *The one everyone longs for.'*

The steps to full-body orgasm

All of the practices you have learnt so far are part of making the shift. Full-body orgasm is not actually just a simple technique that you suddenly switch on! It is a full transformation of so many aspects of your life. Some people discover full-body orgasm as a side effect of personal transformation work or yoga practice. Or people set out to learn it as a technique and then find that their whole life changes!

Tantra 101

You cannot activate full-body orgasm until both your Shiva and Shakti aspects are awakened: your own masculine and feminine aspects in the form of meditative-presence (masculine) and sensitivity to energy (feminine).

At its foundation is a choice. You are making the choice to accept life-force energy into your body, to uplift and animate you and give you a full-bodied experience of the Divine. This means letting go of any patterns that judge, reject or suppress this energy. Having a clear intention accelerates your path, and knowing the kind of resistances you might meet within yourself (old patterns often do not want to let go!) can help with your transformation.

The best way to learn full-body orgasm is through a self-pleasuring meditation. Note the word meditation! We are used to feeling a lot of shame about self-pleasure, and taking it from something you do with guilt into a meditation practice can be quite a jump for some people.

Healing through self-pleasuring

When I first discovered Tantra it was with my partner. He was much more experienced than I was, and I was filled with concerns that I wouldn't be 'Tantric enough' for him! So I went to Mantak's Chia Retreat Centre and completed the women's training there.

Afterwards I went into the mountains alone and rented a little house with a log fire. I made an altar and placed a statue of a goddess, a candle and incense and a few items to honour the Divine. I sat down naked before the altar and began my self-practice.

As I began to massage my breasts with oil, I had a moment of thinking 'I can't sit naked before an altar and massage my breasts'... but then I took a deep breath and continued. I was suddenly moved deeply to tears as I felt my body to be divine. Exactly as it was. There was no separation between divinity and my body, my breasts. My breasts are in fact one of the most divine expressions of this reality!

I felt as if I fell in love with myself at that moment. In a way that was deep reverence for this body as a pure manifestation of the divine source.

I continued my practice, which involved massaging my whole body, stimulating some sexual energy and drawing that energy into a channel called the 'Micro-Cosmic Orbit'.

As the energy began to flow up my spine and through my whole body I felt as if filled with Spirit. I saw the beauty and the innocence of this energy. I felt the energy as a living experience of God within me. My body rocked into a wave-like movement before the altar. I felt so moved that I offered the energy to this Higher Love that I remember as my own essence, to God.

In one evening I completely healed a whole childhood of being told by my society that sex and spirit are completely separate and even at war with one another. Indeed, I discovered that truly they are in love with one another.

Practice: Self-pleasuring meditation

This meditation is about being very aware of how energy feels within your body as you activate it. Therefore, you need to awaken it gently. It is time to leave behind any habits you learned to stimulate yourself hard and fast until you release! You may not want to leave this behind, but the Tantrics promise you there is something much greater beyond it.

If you feel resistant to letting go of the old way, set yourself a task of a 21-day No-Orgasm challenge. We simply have to drop the old way in order to make the space for something else to emerge.

Rather than using self-pleasuring to reach climax, you'll be using gentle massage and touch to awaken your sexual energy into your meditative awareness. You will need to use the breath: by taking a deep breath you can create space around the sensations so that they enter full consciousness.

It can be good to try this sitting up rather than lying down, as this posture creates a heightened sense of awareness.

1. Create your sacred space (*see page 52*), making sure you will not be disturbed. And then consecrate your practice by saying, for example: 'I offer this practice to the Highest Consciousness. May I be guided and protected.'

2. Begin by activating your whole energy. You may want to dance as in the energy activation practices: dancing, shaking and moving your hips. Imagine you are on a date with yourself and take yourself for a great dance!

3. Once you feel alive and in your body, you can take off your clothes (if you haven't already!) and sit in your sacred space.

4. Take a few moments to do Atisha's Heart Meditation (*see page 119*) and open your heart space.

5. Use a natural unscented oil to massage your body with the intention to relax and to awaken your senses.

6. When you feel ready to, you can massage your sexual organs. Remember to be gentle. Massage with a couple of movements then rest your hand over the whole area in stillness and breathe into your sex centre. Close your eyes and watch the sensations.

7. Keep alternating from gently activating movements to holding in stillness and observing. Watch as your energy begins to gather.

8. Do not try to head to climax, but rather think of building a 'chi ball', a ball of energy, at the sex centre.

9. When that ball is about 20 per cent of an orgasm, you can start to inhale it up your spine. It helps to tuck your pelvis in and under, tuck in your belly and slightly tuck in your chin. This flattens the whole spine, making it a smoother passageway for your sexual energy to rise up.

10. Inhale it up to the crown, where you can hold your breath for a moment. See if you can feel the energy gathering at the top of your head.

11. When you are ready to exhale, let the breath flow down the front of your body: from crown to third eye, and down each chakra (*see page 106*) on the front on the body all the way back to your sex centre and root. It helps if you put your tongue on the roof of your mouth.

12. After one or two energy upward draws like this, you can then move into the 'orgasmic wave'. In this you undulate your body in a wave motion, inhaling energy up the spine and exhaling down the front in a continuous cycle.

13. When you are ready to complete, you should no longer feel an accumulation at the sex centre, but feel energy distributed throughout your body or gathered at the crown. At this point, place your hands over your belly and imagine all the energy flowing through you cycling inwards towards your core. Let the energy gather at your core and rest in stillness for a few breaths.

14. This practice will begin to sort your sexual energy habits from rejection and release into acceptance and sublimation. It takes time and you will need to repeat it many times to retrain your energy pathways. After a while of working with 20 per cent of an orgasm you can up the level to 40 per cent and so on, until you can reach 90 per cent (just before the ubiquitous 'point of no return'). Take your time and do not cultivate more energy than you can remain relaxed and present with.

If you keep this practice going, you will find that automatically your lovemaking starts to make a shift. One day you will start to experience full-body orgasms, and as you do then you automatically tend to take your partner with you.

As previously mentioned, this is far greater than just a physical technique and you will also notice that it affects many areas in your life, spirituality, relationships and creativity.

SUMMARY

❖ Tantric orgasm is a well-known aspect of the Tantric path. However, before we start to activate this there are some prerequisites: opening the heart, purification and healing, and opening the energy centres.

❖ Meditation is the foundation of full-body orgasm. This is because presence is the space that holds the energy.

❖ Tantric orgasm is a choice to let life really flow through you. As we feel more energy, we feel more emotions.

❖ It is not only about bringing more energy but releasing our blocks to that energy. This is where the healing around shame and guilt fits in.

❖ You can use self-pleasuring meditation to explore the journey of energy from sex to superconsciousness. This is not the same as masturbation as we know it in society (often a shameful act)... it is taken as a meditation practice in Tantra.

Chapter 16

The Conscious Relationship

*'Relationships are laboratories of the spirit,
or playgrounds for the ego. They can
be heaven or they can be hell. They are
infused with love or infused with fear.'*

MARIANNE WILLIAMSON

When one or both partners in a relationship start to develop Tantric practices, the relationship tends to shift automatically. This is because relationships are about energy flow, so as we change the energy flow within ourselves it shifts also in our relating. If we have places we are blocked within, then this affects our relating. Ultimately, healthy relating is about creating a foundational healthy relationship within yourself. This can then be shared with another.

Relationship is about commitment. But not about committing to each other's personalities, nor about making a promise to feel the same way forever, happily ever after. These commitments would be impossible to keep in the long term and one would have to violate the Higher Truth to keep them. Rather, it is about commitment to love itself. When two people make a commitment to love in their relating, then this can carry them through moments of not-love in a way that supports healing and transformation.

There are many forms that a relationship might take, and Tantra does not seek to specify how that should look. Some Tantrics have monogamous long-term relationships; some have open relationships; others may flow more from one connection to another, having a primary relationship with themselves.

> *It isn't the form of the relationship that's important but the intention and the underlying principles that hold it in place.*

A relationship is an ideal opportunity to cultivate transfiguration, the Tantric principle of seeing the truth within another (*see page 95*). This is not just about eye-gazing to soft music, although such a practice is an immense support (*see page 57*). It is about bringing all that we have gained from our Tantra practice into the challenging moments, and choosing to respond from love rather than from patterns of defence and attack. Thus a Tantric relationship gives us the opportunity to learn about unconditional love.

It is important to remember that Tantra concerns all relationships, not only the sexual ones. Every relationship we have is a reflection of ourselves and an indication of where we are at in life. Every relationship invites us to learn about love. If you have difficulty entering intimate relationships, start by focusing on the everyday relationships you encounter, from your family to the people you work with, including the shopkeeper whom you have a three-minute interaction with – every relating is an opportunity to practise love.

Exercise: Your current relationship status

Before looking at how to move into deeper relationship, it's a good idea to stop and assess where you are. What aspects about your relating do you like, and what aspects do you feel an inner calling to shift?

❖ What are the best relationships in your life? Is it a sexual relationship, or with friends or with family members? List the great relationships you have and then ask yourself what makes them so great.

❖ How many difficult or unresolved relationships do you have in your life? Take the time to list the names of the people so that you can take a look at what still needs to be healed or resolved. Try to avoid judgement of yourself or of them.

❖ What are the biggest recurring issues that arise in your relationships? Write them down so that you can see them.

❖ What conflicts arise for you? Are there places you feel you have to compromise or make a difficult choice?

❖ How are you with communication? Do you find it easy to approach challenges? Do you avoid them? Do you often end up in conflict?

❖ What are your intentions for your intimate relationships? What is the purpose for you? Do you dedicate your relationships to anything?

❖ How does love manifest in your life? Do you find it easier to give or to receive? What do you think holds you back from love?

❖ How do most of your relationships end? If you have difficulty even starting them, what seems to get in the way?

Use this as a guide for your own contemplation and self-reflection so that you get a tune-in of where you are at in your life with relating.

Creating a conscious relationship

What does it mean to commit to love? It is about making a conscious choice, and then living it out to the best of your abilities. That means choosing love and then in moments in which we are tempted to act or speak from non-love we remember our commitment and choose otherwise. It is basically a choice between ego-based reality and love-based reality. When fear arises, do we try to defend it with ego defences or do we choose to open our hearts? This is the simple key behind creating a conscious relationship. It is simple, but not always so easy!

The trouble is that our egoic defences are so deeply ingrained that we often don't notice when they arise. Often we don't realize that those defence patterns are not who we really are. In the moment, we tend to identify totally with the egoic defences and then we enter conflict or separation. This identification with ego is called 'attachment'. As this attachment can be so strong, we need to commit to love in order to be able to let go of the temptation to act out our egoic patterns.

It can be helpful to consider how the ego might arise in relating versus what the conscious alternative might look like. Awareness is the first step to help us to make a change. You can look at it as a choice of who is running the relationship show – is it your ego calling the shots or is it your soul, your true nature? So often we say that we are looking for a soulmate, but if we are looking from the ego-self then we will never meet soul to soul.

> *'Ego says: Once everything falls into place, I'll feel peace...*
> *Spirit says: Find your peace, and then everything will fall into place.'*
> MARIANNE WILLIAMSON

The conscious relationship guide

Use the following list to recognize, in different relationship situations, if you have a tendency to come from ego-self or from soul-self.

Intention

❖ **Ego:** Is waiting for someone to come and save them or make life better in some way. The ego looks for a relationship to serve them, fulfil their needs and makes things better.

❖ **Soul:** Calls in the relationship that serves each other's highest purpose and truth.

Searching

❖ **Ego:** Makes a list of all of the characteristics that they think the other person should have.

❖ **Soul:** Meets each new person as they are and finds many things to appreciate in the other. The soul-self is open to the mystery of discovering the new through the other.

Connection

- ❖ **Ego:** Presents an image of who they think they should be to attract a partner. The ego-self creates a persona that it has come to believe will make them desirable. The ego-self presents itself through posturing.

- ❖ **Soul:** Meets authentically in each living moment, no matter how vulnerable that might be.

Desires

- ❖ **Ego:** What can I get from this relationship?

- ❖ **Soul:** What can I give to this relationship?

Blame

- ❖ **Ego:** When something 'goes wrong' the ego blames the other person in some way.

- ❖ **Soul:** When some challenge arises, the soul-self owns their part in it as deeply as they can.

Communication

- ❖ **Ego:** Says, 'You.'

- ❖ **Soul:** Says, 'I.'

Default

- ❖ **Ego:** Complains and nags as a default.

- ❖ **Soul:** Expresses gratitude and praise as a default.

Countenance

- **Ego:** Can be cruel.
- **Soul:** Is kind.

Essence

- **Ego:** Has hard edges, rigidity.
- **Soul:** There is a softness about the soul-self, a flowing nature.

Focus

- **Ego:** Goal-orientated.
- **Soul:** Process-orientated.

Meeting fear

- **Ego:** When fear arises the ego-self feels that it has to defend itself or attack the other.
- **Soul:** When fear arises the soul-self opens the heart in order to make space to hold that fear within loving presence.

Response

- **Ego:** Ego-self rises very fast into reaction.
- **Soul:** Takes a deep breath and takes the time to respond.

Commitment

❖ **Ego:** When a challenge arises, the ego-self thinks everything has gone wrong and is ready to walk out the door. The ego-self is faithless because it is founded on fear.

❖ **Soul:** When a challenge arises, the soul-self has faith in a greater love and is prepared to do whatever needs to be done to return the situation to love.

Letting go

❖ **Ego:** Holds resentments and lists of all the things the other has done wrong. When the list gets big enough, they often leave that relationship and all they remember is that big long list of faults. They can use this list to justify the end of the relationship ('It's all the fault of the other). They might let go of the other person, but they take all of the pain with them in the form of their resentments.

❖ **Soul:** Forgives. The soul-self can forgive all actions of the other that were not from love, because the soul-self knows the true nature of the other. The soul-self knows that any non-loving actions or words came from fear. Instead of judgement upon the visible actions, they have compassion for that underlying fear. From this compassionate space they forgive all that is not love. If they move on from a relationship all they remember is the love.

Subtleties

❖ **Ego:** Would use this list to analyse their partner or their ex, and decide how much their partner is coming from ego!

❖ **Soul:** Would use this list to better understand themselves and bring awareness to where their own ego patterns might be arising. The soul-self would not use this list as ammunition against their partner!

Use this guide to help bring awareness to which part of you is running the show at any one time! When a problem arises we tend to go looking deep into the issue itself and try to pick it apart and understand it. However, it is more effective to look at the seed of the event: what part of us has created this? Anything seeded from ego-self will grow pain and separation. Anything seeded from soul-self will grow love and harmony. So if you don't find peace and happiness in your relationship, take a look at the seed of your choices, and choose otherwise.

However, understanding and awareness are often not enough. Our own daily practices can really help us to begin to drop old ego-self habits and move towards living from our soul-self or true nature. Also when you have your own practices then you do not need to process everything that arises together with your partner, as sometimes one person in a relationship can resolve a discord on their own.

Other times, however, it can be helpful to have some relating tools and communication skills to move through disharmony back to peace together. It's an absolute wonder that these things are not taught in schools, as few things could be more useful in life than relationship skills. Luckily, the spiritual scene is now abundant with guidance. Here are a few tools based upon Tantric principles.

Relationship tools for one

It is always worth developing your toolkit for moving through any unloving moments. Your partner may not always be open or available for processing with you. Sometimes in moments of conflict, the other may be tempted to pull away. At other times something comes up within you that you could easily turn into a big problem or issue if you take it straight to your partner. If you work to move some energy and emotion first on your own, oftentimes the problem reduces or even disappears! Then you can have more time with your beloved having fun together and less time dealing with issues.

Move energy

If you feel very angry, frustrated, annoyed or any other active emotion, the best thing to do is to move some energy. Go for a run. Put on your headphones and shake your body or dance. Clasp your hands together and pretend you are chopping wood between your legs (a qigong move called 'the woodcutter'). Bash a pillow (a classic). Jump up and down shouting, 'Hoo!' So often we can move these emotions with a cathartic movement and sound rather than channelling them into harsh and angry words towards our partner. Always think to discharge the energy from a strong active emotion rather than direct that charged emotion onto another person.

Go into nature

Never underestimate the healing power of nature. Take yourself for a long walk alone in a place in nature to 'air out' any circulating issues in your mind. Try to find a walk with a great view where you can sit and take a different perspective. There is a reason so many ancient sages used to climb up a mountain to ponder life...

Meditate

Healing a conflict is often just a shift in perception. We get so attached to our own perspective and sense of being right (the other person, therefore, being wrong). It is the mind that needs to be healed. When the mind gets attached to a certain position, then we start to see a reality that is projected out of that state of mind. It feels as if what we see is showing us the 'truth', but actually what we are thinking is creating our reality. Thus we get stuck in repeating cycles of the same issues.

The solution is to learn to meditate. Meditation is the discipline of letting go of attachment to thoughts and choosing to shift attention to something else, such as the breath. When we take time to shift focus away from thoughts, we open to the possibility of expanding beyond our limited perception. All we need is the willingness to see things otherwise and to take a few minutes to sit back from our thoughts.

Forgive

Being willing to forgive your partner is being willing to remember that their true nature is love and all unloving actions are not who they are. It is not only about accepting harmful behaviour towards us, but also letting go of resentment. We may need to move away from our partner in a heated moment, but doing so with the intention to forgive is a way to heal what has arisen. All of your heart practices and meditations support this process.

Pray

Prayer is not so popular these days as people move away from traditional religions. The idea of desperately pleading with a distant God for help may feel disempowering to some people. However, if you acknowledge that there is a Higher Truth – a reality that is love – then you know when you have fallen out of it because you are experiencing something that is not love.

To pray is to speak from the small-self, the ego-self to that Higher Self, to the Ultimate Truth. To ask to return to that higher love once more. It is like setting a very strong intention and asking the universe to support you. Prayer is also a form of surrender in which you let go of trying to fix it all yourself, and instead ask the universe to restore truth once more.

In Tantric metaphysics, Shakti can become cut off from Shiva her lover. The energy that creates your life experience can become cut off from the higher consciousness. When this happens there is an experience of pain, confusion and suffering. Shakti calls out to her lover, 'Oh Shiva! I have become lost from you. Please bring me home to your Truth that I may remember myself as love!' Only when the two lovers are united again can peace reign.

So to pray is to ask for help from a higher force because you are humble enough to acknowledge that you have strayed from truth and have entered suffering.

Practice: Simple prayers

Setting a strong intention and surrendering to higher forces is a very powerful way to get your ego-self out of the way and receive the blessings of healing. The Universal Truth is much more powerful than all of the untruths that arise. Surrendering to that Universal Truth is much faster than trying to nit-pick your way through each untruth, attempting to fix each one. Why not go straight to the Source with prayer? A simple prayer you can use is:

'Great Spirit (Highest Truth/Shiva/God/Universe, etc.),

I offer up all of this pain and confusion to you. I offer up all of the energy around this situation. I am willing to change my perception. Please help me see otherwise. Help me to see the truth and feel the love. Please use me to heal this situation. I am willing to open my heart.

Aho/Amen/Om Shanti.'

Such a prayer is about calling to your Higher Self, to the Ultimate Truth, and offering up all that is not-love. You can make your prayer even more powerful by combining it with an energy-raising practice that you learnt in Chapter 13, such as shaking (*see page 149*) or sounding (*see page 147*).

If you find yourself stuck in a situation in which you cannot see beyond your projections and judgements on your partner, you can also use prayer:

'Great Spirit (Highest Truth/Shiva/God/Universe, etc.),

I am angry with [insert name] because [insert reason].
Please take my judgement from me. I am willing to
see things differently. Please replace my judgement
with compassion and true seeing. Please help me
to open my heart to [insert name] once more.

Aho/Amen/Om Shanti.'

Relationship tools for two

It is a huge support to any relationship if both partners are willing to engage in healing processes together when things get challenging. It is best to agree on what processes you will use *before* you need to use them. It can be very provocative if you're in the middle of a heated argument and someone tries to impose a Gestalt session or a particular sharing structure, as the chances are, the ego will feel too threatened in that moment to agree to that.

However, if you chat it over whilst things are calm and there are no defences up, then you can agree what you will do in a challenge. It's a bit like sorting out the fire escape strategy whilst there is no fire. It's not that you want an argument or a fire, but you want to make sure you have the healthiest response possible should it arise!

Couples can cause some serious wounds to the relationship with words spoken harshly in heated moments. It is definitely better to find ways to avoid creating those scars in the first place. Though few relationships stay rosy 24/7, you don't have to live with conflict as an expected part of relating. A mature relationship has love as its baseline and cleans up all non-love as effectively as possible.

Intention

It is powerful for a couple to set a shared intention for the relationship. This is stating one's commitment to love. Hearing that out loud from your partner can then help in challenging moments, as you remember that the intention is for love. This makes it easier not to react to the ego-self, as you remember the soul-self that is committed to love. To offer a relationship in service to the Divine or to the highest love is a form of consecration, thus making the relationship a sacred space.

True listening

This is an absolute non-negotiable factor for a harmonious relationship. We are so afraid of rejection that we often shut down our ability to listen when our partner is upset. However, people who are not heard tend to speak louder (and often more harshly) or pull away and separate from the other. So true listening is a vital skill in relating.

There are several keys to listening. One is to relax. Taking a deep breath with a big sigh on the out-breath helps to put us in a more receptive state. A strange phenomenon is that we unconsciously squeeze our anus when we are not really taking in someone's words. So I have a catchphrase 'relax your anus and listen!'

But perhaps the most effective tool for true listening is the art of repeating back what you just heard, as accurately as possible. This is much more effective than reacting or defending, as the ego-self would have us do.

> **Partner 1:** 'I can't stand it when you come in late and make so much noise that you wake me up.'

> **Partner 2 (not listening):** *'Well you wake me up in the mornings when you get up to do yoga.'*

Or

> *'What are you talking about? I'm really quiet when I come in. You must have a problem with sleeping. My last partner was never disturbed.'*

> **Partner 1:** 'I can't stand it when you come in late and make so much noise that you wake me up.'

> **Partner 2:** *'What I hear you say is that you can't stand it when I come in late and make so much noise that I wake you up.'*

This simple tool of listening and repeating back has the effect of discharging the emotional charge that the speaker is carrying. Once the charge has calmed down then you are both in a better place to discuss what solution can be made. Always aim to discharge the emotional charge before making decisions or action plans. If you try to resolve things whilst emotions are still hot, then any plan made will be tainted with that charge. Make plans and decisions from peace, not from charge.

Tantra 101

Never end a relationship from a charged-up place: 'That's it! I'm leaving! [*slammed door*].' You may be leaving the relationship, but you take the pain with you if you do it this way. If you feel you have to leave the situation make it temporary: 'I'm sorry I need to step out and take space from this right now. I'll come back when I feel more centred.' Then make decisions together once you have come to peace. If you make decisions out of anger you will have to reap the fruits of that. If you make decisions from a peaceful place, you will bear peaceful fruits in your life.

Conscious communication

True listening is the core of conscious communication. The next step is to bring awareness to your words and aim to own your feelings.

Conscious communication is often a simple matter of using the word 'I' and not the word 'you'.

'You are so loud and noisy at night. You are so inconsiderate. You're one of the most selfish people I know. You stay out late and then wake me up. I can't live with you!'

Versus:

'I am feeling disturbed because I wake up when you come in late. I don't want to stop you having your own schedule, but I feel that I need a good night's sleep. I am wondering if we can consider different possibilities so that we can find the way for you to have your flexibility and for me to get my sleep.'

When our partner owns their feelings and emotions, it is much easier to hear them than when they attack us with them. It is emotionally unsafe when people attack others with emotional charge, and it creates a relationship in which neither partner feels safe keeping their heart open. Thus if we want to live in love, we have to bring awareness to this habit and choose otherwise.

> *We cannot make love happen, but we can create the space in which love flourishes.*

Tantra 101

If you want to delve deeper into conscious communication, then explore the system of 'non-violent communication'. It is really worth joining a course together as a couple. This is like taking the fire safety course together, and hopefully reducing the risk of even starting a fire in the first place!

Wrestling

You might think this is a joke after talking about conscious communication and non-violence, but actually there is a valid place for moving energy together. I am not suggesting having a punch-up, but engaging in a play-fight can be a superb way to discharge tension. Most conflict is connected to some blocked energy somewhere along the way. Sometimes we can talk our way out of conflict, and sometimes we need to move energy in the body.

A great way is to press your hands together against your partner's, whilst looking in your partner's eyes. Stand strongly rooted on the ground, one leg in front of the other, and take a deep inhale together. As you exhale, push your hands against your partner's, making a sound on the out-breath (often it sounds something like 'arrgghhh!' or a growl). Keep eye contact throughout. This is not about pushing harder than your partner or pushing them over, just finding the meeting point in your pressure. Afterwards release your hands and just look in each other's eyes.

Another alternative is a play-fight like two kittens or puppies. Pushing against each other and rolling around on the floor or the bed. But make sure you stay very conscious and present with your partner so that you do not hurt them. This is play only. Many animals engage in play-fighting to stay healthy and happy together.

Wrestling back to love

I went through a stage when I was experiencing a lot of frustration in life and especially in my relationship. It was manifesting physically, as my menstrual periods came along with extra tension. A great qigong teacher observed me and said: 'You need to wrestle.' As soon as he said it, I felt the shift inside. YES!

My lover and I went home and started to play-fight on the bed, growling and pushing against each other. It felt so great that we didn't even stop when one of the legs of the bed broke! We tumbled onto the floor and continued. Giggles started to come between growls. In the end we fell into a heap in each other's arms. I was crying with relief. He held me in his loving embrace and we had returned to love. My periods started to get better too!

Raising energy together

When things feel stuck, a great thing to do is to move the energy. Putting on some music and shaking or dancing can really shift things. If you both practise Tantric breathwork, then you could choose to use a meditation together (*see page 35*). Another great thing to do is to go out to a Five Rhythms or Ecstatic Dance class in your area. These are designed to let you move energy. You will come home feeling renewed and often a whole load of apparent problems are gone after a good dance. It is not about denial of a problem, but the problem often shifts because the energy has been moved.

I heard about a teacher called Mama Gena who had people share their problems whilst being touched and caressed sensually. I tried it with a friend and we developed the practice of 'orgasmic problem-solving'. Problems are actually made out of being in a state of contraction, so if we are willing to move into expansion then the problem falls away or reduces. It is about shifting our perception of reality, and when we move from contraction to expansion that shift happens.

Of course making love is a good way to raise energy, but often we don't feel like it when we are in conflict! (A good friend of mine says, 'F**k first; talk later!'). We may not feel open enough to make love in the midst of conflict (in which case try one of the above suggestions first).

Healthy lovemaking is a great way to avoid conflicts arising in the first place. Making love can shift a lot of potential problems; it keeps the energy moving and helps prevent blocks from forming. Tantric lovemaking is very good to bring harmony and connection to a relationship. So much can be moved between the couple on the subtle level and avoid it turning into a problem in our relationship.

Tantra 101

A relationship is nourished by deep intimacy. When we do not have true intimate moments then a sense of separation can start to set into a relationship like mould in a room that is not aired. Creating sacred space to drop in together is so vital to support living in love (*see also page 52*).

Practice: Belly to belly – embodied intimacy

Tantra teacher David Cates has distilled over three decades of experience in the field of Tantra into a simple process that is known affectionately by those who use it as 'belly to belly'.

In this process, the couple lie down face to face, and indeed belly to belly, on a bed or mattress. They find a way to have physical connection that feels authentic in that moment – whether that is fingertips lightly touching or a more full-bodied embrace.

Then they drop in by taking deep breaths and sighing together. This is the foundation of the whole practice – a form of Tantric sounding (*see page 147*).

The most common form is to take three breaths: into the heart, into the belly and into the sexual organs. Each and every breath has a big and loud sigh on the out-breath. You can do three with eyes open and then try three with eyes closed.

You might then want to spend some time in this embrace, simply breathing together and listening to the sound of each other's breath. After 10 minutes or so, open you eyes and take 5 minutes each to share how you feel in that moment.

In David Cates' circles there are then many variations of this practice, including eye contact, sounding, touching, sharing and other forms of intimate connection. But the advanced variations are best with a facilitator holding space for them.

Crossing the sacred line

I have spent some time observing what makes us reactive, defensive or attacking to our partner. Upon investigation, I came up with a theory that I call the 'sacred line'. In other words, there is a place within each of us that is our business and only our business. There is a deep vulnerable wound-core, which is all of the life lessons unique to us. These lessons can help us awaken if we choose.

No one else can do our inner work
for us – not even our partner!
Especially not our partner!

It is tempting in relationships to point out the other person's issues. In fact sometimes it is frustrating if our partner can't see their blind spots. If only we could just point them out!

But the thing is, that this deep vulnerable wound-core is exactly that: a vulnerable wound. If you had a physical wound and someone poked their finger in it, you would recoil and defend yourself or push them away. And so it is with our emotional and psychological wounds. If someone pokes their finger in it, we react – this is 'crossing the sacred line'. Often when you see your partner react, you poke even harder to try and fix their reaction too. The situation gets worse and worse!

A lot of psychological violence is caused by such interactions. Often each partner is only trying to help, but it is really not helpful. If you see your beloved start to get defensive, the best thing you can do is to notice and ask yourself how you can facilitate their relaxation and opening. We do not open someone by trying to force them open, but by holding a loving present space that they feel safe within.

Always ask: *how can I help my beloved feel relaxed and open in my presence?*

If you notice that you've crossed the sacred line, then back off and apologize for crossing the boundary. A genuine apology and ability to see where you overstepped the mark can help rebuild trust.

Every time you cross the sacred line, you will damage the trust and safety of the relationship. Over time, this can create such a deep separation between the two people that the whole relationship falls apart. We always need to try to build trust, and take care to make reparations with genuine apologies if we see that we have damaged it.

Even though we long to relate and find union with one another, we also all have a sovereign self. Sovereignty is not about having a separate self, but having a unique self: each of us a unique ray of the sun, a unique expression of one same source. This sovereignty needs to be respected: respect that your beloved is on their own path, and though you may walk side by side for part of that journey you cannot do the walk for them.

Transfiguration and forgiveness

Forgiveness is the act that helps us shift from separation to love. It is an essential part of our transformation around love and relating. When we hold on to resentments we are holding on to an untrue reality and making it real. When we forgive, we are letting go of all that was not from love. Instead we look at the love that is trapped beneath the actions.

Remember the ego-self is a form of defence. So when it arises in yourself or your beloved, you can remember that there is some sort of fear and vulnerability appearing. If you can see below the ego-self to the fear and vulnerability, then suddenly you will feel your heart switch from separation and judgement to compassion and love.

*If you remember that everything is
either love or it is distorted love, you
will start to see the world differently
– with a lot more compassion.*

To see the essence of love within all is called 'transfiguration' and is one of the core principles and practices in Tantra. It is easy to see love when it is expressed purely, but when it is distorted it is harder to see. We are usually tempted to identify the other person by their words and actions and we lose sight of their true self in that moment. If someone is shouting and swearing at you, you may see this as being who they are. But if you choose to practice transfiguration, then try the following steps:

1. Remind yourself that this is distorted love.

2. Look for the fear hidden beneath their words and actions.

3. When you see that fear, your heart will start to open automatically. At this point send love to the fear.

4. If you cannot sense the fear, try Atisha's Heart Meditation, breathing in their pain, and breathing out love (*see page 119*). Alternatively, pray that your perception be altered.

5. Once you feel their vulnerability that is being defended, forgive the defence, the ego-self. Know that it is only trying to protect a part that feels vulnerable.

6. The only thing that can help their vulnerability to feel safe enough to drop the ego-defence is love. If you feel their fear with an open heart, then you are supporting them to be in their true self.

Remember this process is not about pointing out your partner's defence or analysing them. If we are analysed in a vulnerable moment we will only put up even more defences. It is completely counterproductive to analyse, so try to avoid this temptation. Only love can make their vulnerability feel safe. Your clever mind telling them what's wrong with them will not make them feel safe but have the opposite effect!

Self-transfiguration

You can also use these principles for yourself. In moments when you see yourself in ego-self, try to look within and find where your fear and vulnerability are. Instead of speaking from ego-self, share with your partner what is making you feel vulnerable. Before you share, ask them to hold space for you so that they know that you want to be heard, and not analysed or fixed.

If you slipped for a moment and spoke from ego-self, as soon as you see this, own it. Go to your partner and say: 'I'm sorry I said [...] I was defending my fear. Please forgive me.' This is a fast way to keep things clear in a relationship. Own it. Clear it.

Creating a supportive relationship

Transfiguration is basically a way to support one another in becoming your true selves and acting from your soul-self. If you choose to use it in relationships, then your relationships will become potent vehicles for spiritual growth. Projections will reduce, pain and conflict lessen, and you will live together in more peace and joy.

Transfiguration does make space for making mistakes. After all we are human and cannot expect ourselves or our partner to live in 100 per cent enlightened perfection all of the time! But there is an awareness of ego-self, and understanding that ego-self is innocent and only trying to protect vulnerability. As we forgive one another's ego-actions, we make it safer and safer to be in the vulnerability of having an open heart. Healing happens automatically, as our fears are one by one brought to love.

A relationship lived in this way is completely different from the old model in which we expect the other person to make us happy.

*A Tantric relationship becomes a precious
vehicle for our healing, growth and love.*

SUMMARY

❖   Relationships can take many forms. A conscious relationship is not about the form but the underlying principles that it is based upon.

❖   In Tantra, a couple might chose to commit to love or to God, rather than to each other's personalities.

❖   A relationship can be used as a reflection to see where we are living from ego (fear) and where we are living our soul's truth (love).

❖   We may need tools to work through challenges within a relationship. A relationship is work in progress! There are many ways to help remove the barriers to love as they arise.

❖   Communication is a large part of relating, so learning some conscious communication tools is a huge aid to a peaceful and evolving relationship.

❖   Transfiguration is an ancient Tantric practice that can really assist us in transforming a normal relationship into a spiritual relationship, as well as bringing us home to a greater love.

Chapter 17
Moving from Karma to Dharma

'When Dharma is present, it feels as if we are acting in complete accord with the universe. It is as if a powerful unseen force is sustaining our efforts, endowing them with potency.'

SIMON HAAS, *THE BOOK OF DHARMA*

We are creating our own reality. Ideally we want to create the reality that is in alignment with our true nature and thus create our true path. This true path is called our 'dharma'. Dharma is living truth – not simply awakening in one moment to our true nature, but living it out. This is our higher purpose.

When we live our higher purpose, life flows with ease and grace. All that we do is harmonious with all that is going on around us. Life is filled with a sense of meaningfulness, but not from some external achievement: the meaningfulness of living as love.

But we do not always create our true reality. We have a choice each moment and we can also choose to create separation. This is the choice of the ego-self, and we are often tempted to make this choice out of a sense of self-protection. This protection is false and only separates us. However, when we are afraid we may choose to protect with our ego's defences.

You can see that you have two seeds that can each create a different reality. The ego-self seed creates what is called 'karma'. This word literally means 'effect' and describes the effects created by acting from our ego-self. When we act from ego-self we affect those whom we relate with also, and thus a whole reality is formed. It is inevitable there will be some element of pain and suffering, as the results of the separation that the ego-self creates.

You can use your relationships as a mirror to see if you are acting from ego-self or soul-self. If your relationships are disharmonious then it is time to look within and see where you have made an egoic choice. Then you can choose otherwise and bring yourself back to your dharma. This will create harmony and love in your relationships. Dharma is living a life of service, but not being submissive by serving other people's egos. Dharma is about being in the service of love.

Living in karma keeps us smaller than we really are. The ego-self is made up of defences and shields, so there is really no room for your true soul to shine within it. Living in dharma allows us to be the true self that we came here to be: a being of love, radiating that love and pouring it into every word and action.

Shifting karma with Tantric practices

Karmic healing is known to be one of the most challenging kinds. Habits can be really sticky, and even when we see them sometimes we still cannot overcome them.

Tantra says that we can shift karma by raising energy. This is because the sexual energy holds the ancestral codes within it. Our sexual energy is the energy of reproduction, which gets passed along the ancestral lines. It contains the genetic codes for our make-up, and the theory goes that the karmic energy is also encoded here.

This implies that if you're not healing your unhealthy patterns and conditioning, then you may pass on any unresolved karma to the next generation. They then have to deal with these issues throughout their lifetime too – either suffering from the karma or perhaps engaging in some sort of healing or practice that begins to shift the patterns.

With Tantric practice, the energy sublimation described in Chapter 14 (*see page 153*) actually lifts the sexual energy to a high enough vibration that old patterns can fall away. This uplifting of energy is seen as a catalyst for healing, which the Taoists call 'inner alchemy'. If we want to change the form of a substance, one way is by heating it up. If we raise up the sexual energy, it becomes lighter and expands, and it is possible to shift stubborn habits and beliefs. In this way we can move into embodying our true nature, unencumbered by old patterns and habits that would keep us small.

Practice: Sex magic – raising energy with intention

Sex magic is the practice of using sexual energy to power up your highest intentions. At the simplest level, this is done by setting an intention and then raising the energy.

Making love with your beloved is one method to raise energy, but you can also use any practice that uplifts energy. For example:

❖ Chakra Flow: It is especially potent to raise energy up one chakra at a time, from root to crown (*see page 106*). This might be by Osho's Chakra Breathing Meditation™, which moves through each chakra in order for three cycles.

❖ Dancing: preferably starting more connected to the earth and your feet and working the energy up into the heart and crown (*see page 149*).

❖ Ecstatic shaking: allowing the body to shake off all limitations you have felt around your vision and expanding into your full potential (*see page 149*).

❖ Making love: at first like wild animals or an earthy lover (*see page 176*), and then moving through each elemental style until you arrive at the more subtle level together. At the subtle stage, move into yab-yum posture, the woman (or smaller partner) sits in the man's lap (*see page 53*). Let all the energy rise to the third eye and crown.

It is important that when you work with intention, you are in alignment with your higher self or true nature. If you use energy to set an intention that comes from your ego-self, you will grow your ego! The ego-self creates a sense of separation and suffering, so you will create more suffering for yourself in the long term.

Using consecration is a way to align with your higher self (dedicate your practice to the Highest).

1. Take some quiet time alone to tune in to any suffering in your life that you might want to heal. Or you may tune in to your highest calling: what is your heart's desire, your soul's calling?

2. Simplify this into a clear positive intention. For example, 'I want to get rid of this painful knee' becomes 'I want to feel a healthy, flexible knee.'

3. Choose your energy-raising activity (see ideas above). If it is an activity you are sharing with someone else, then share your intentions together.

4. Before the activity, make a consecration such as, 'I offer this energy to Highest Consciousness. I visualize my knee healthy and flexible, if that is Divine Will. May this [*dance/meditation/lovemaking, etc.*] be blessed. May my knee be blessed.' It is very important always to align with divine will. Using energy to create against divine will won't ever serve your highest purpose and can create negative effects in your life (aka 'bad karma').

5. During the activity, visualize the energy flowing upwards to your crown, carrying your prayers and intentions upwards. When you feel really expanded and open, reconnect with your intention as if it has already happened. Have gratitude for your healing.

6. After the peak of energy, be open to receive blessings. Let yourself relax and rest and become receptive. If you danced or exercised, lie down on the floor in stillness. If you made love, lie intertwined with your lover and rest.

Tantric master Margot Anand has created a whole system around using lovemaking to power up intentions. You can find out more about this in her book *The Art of Sexual Magic*.

Shaking my way through divorce

By far one of the most challenging times of my life was the completion of a nine-year relationship and marriage. A relationship that had once served our growth was now stilting our expansion and I knew that if I wanted to keep growing spiritually I had to let go.

In the process of ending such a long and intimate relationship, many emotions surfaced as well as awareness of old patterns. I decided to take myself to a shaking ashram in Bali to facilitate the healing process.

The spiritual centre was led by Energy Master Ratu Bagus, who led the practice of shaking to techno music: nine hours a day in three-hour blocks. This was some serious shaking!

This practice was one of the strongest practices for raising energy I have ever encountered. From 6 a.m. every day I dragged myself to the temple space to shake my wearing body and resistant psyche! Throughout the temple there were buckets for spitting and even vomiting into, as the old blocked emotions shifted. It was a really bizarre scene but some powerful healing happens there. I met people who had incredible results healing serious long-term diseases, as well as those working on emotions.

Thus I entered one of the most powerful purifications and transformations of my life. After several weeks of raising energy and clearing old restrictions, a pattern emerged. I would start a session feeling resistance or even physical pain. Then I would start to shake and recite the mantras. I would begin shaking the resistance, shaking my anger or frustration or other negative emotions. But over the shaking session these would begin to open up and transform into energy. I would become flooded with feelings of joy and ecstasy. By the end I would be in a prayer of gratitude.

This ashram does not consider itself to be Tantric because it is of a Balinese Hindu lineage; however, as a Tantrika myself I took it as a powerful kundalini practice and Tantric purification. I am sure that the practice took months, if not years, off the recovery process from ending the relationship. I soon found that I was free of resentments, attachments and stories, and was able to move on in my life, in peace and with an open heart.

I later learned to use consecration in all of my dance, chanting and lovemaking. Dedicating all of my energy-raising practices to my Higher Self, to the Divine and to the healing of the world. This made the most profound shift from experiencing ecstasy for more personal pleasure, to experiencing ecstasy as full-bodied prayer. It had powerful effects on my life, supporting my transition into my true life-purpose, alignment with divine will and ease and flow of creating and manifesting. When you start to step into offering your divinely intended gifts, then the whole universe supports you!

Conscious community

When we move into conscious relationships, it is not only about our sexual relationships. We are part of a whole web of interconnectedness. It is not just about finding love with one person, but with every person with whom we interact. The highest attainment in Tantra is to see the divine nature in everyone, and to act from that truth. That means acting from love with your bus driver, your work colleagues – and even with the parking attendant who issues you with a parking ticket!

You can think of your intimate relationship as the place that you practise love and learn love. But there is no point in learning love if you do not apply it to every experience in your life.

I have a phrase I like to apply to all of my interactions, which is: 'May I leave each person I interact with better off than when I found them.'

I like to leave even small interactions, like with a shopkeeper or bank teller, feeling warm in my heart, and feeling them happier for having interacted with me. Every interaction is an opportunity for love. Maybe the checkout girl has had a bad day and feels upset about an argument she had with her boyfriend. But if you see beyond her defences and mood and say 'good morning' to that place within her that is love, you can be part of what supports her back to her truth.

Being love is not about trying hard to be loving. It is more about holding a perception and acting from there. Seeing the truth within others is in itself a gift of love. Forgiving others their non-loving behaviours is in itself a gift of love. Choosing to stay in your soul-self even when someone comes at you from their ego-self – this is in itself a great gift of love.

Tantric practices help people to activate the energy body. As we raise our energy, we replace defence patterns with the energy body. We no longer need to hold defence patterns to feel safe, as our energy body creates a natural protection (or aura). Defences make us feel separate from one another, but energy connects us. Our energy does not stop at our physical skin, it radiates out and interconnects with energy around us. Thus we feel interconnected with all of life.

When many people practise Tantra in one community, then a miracle starts to emerge. Many people living with awakened energy bodies start to connect on this subtle level. People feel connected – a feeling sometimes described as 'oneness'. You cannot do harm to another once you know the truth of your interconnectedness, for to hurt another is to hurt yourself.

There is a creative energy running through the community that allows people to be authentic and spontaneous, living from spirit. A strong creative energy makes a very alive community, and shared creativity holds community together. Creativity is an expression of love so sharing creative expression is a way to share love.

People often think that Tantric communities must be one big orgy. In a way it is true – everyone *is* making love together. But it is not about sex. It is about making love through every interaction. Making love through sharing. Making love through music. Making love through dance.

Tantra is inviting us to relearn how to love and then to live as that love.

Creating a Tantric community

I set myself a quest: to find out how we can live Tantra and create the same lifestyle as I've found in Tantric workshops and festivals. In these places magical communities are formed but these events come and go, so I decided to start a community that fully embodies Tantra and created 'LiveTantra'.

I invited a number of Tantra teachers to live together in a villa in Southeast Asia and our shared creative project was to create an online platform for Tantra but more important was that the project was our own community.

We shared morning practices every day. We co-created our project. When conflict or challenge arose in the creative process, we used relationship tools to process and heal it. We ran evening events such as Tantric rituals, ecstatic dance and other practices.

We had a balance between private time, group time and one-on-one time. We had a balance between work and play. We would pause business meetings when they got too heady and have a dance break!

This project has been so rewarding and such a great opportunity for growth that it has continued. We now meet several times a year for LiveTantra community events. The depth of love and trust that has developed in many of us is now a foundation for teaching together at events around the world. By living and practising love, we are able to share that authentically with others.

SUMMARY

❖ Dharma is our true path, or highest purpose. Our whole life flows with ease and grace when we are living our Dharma.

❖ Karma is created when we are living from ego and unconscious patterns: we weave a web of life around us that may contain problems, separation and pain.

❖ There are Tantric practices, sometimes known as 'sex magic' that use sexual energy as the fuel to activate our highest purpose.

❖ When many people start to live their highest truth, then a unified field is generated. It is a field of creativity and love.

Conclusion:
How Could Tantra
Serve the World?

*'[Tantra] is probably the only spiritual path
that excludes nothing and no one, and,
in this way, it corresponds to the deep
aspirations of men and women today.'*

DANIEL ODIER

In these times of massive unrest, chaos and confusion, worldwide, spiritual awakening cannot be limited to a mere personal journey of enlightenment. We are not in this alone. The concept of enlightenment tends to conjure up images of a lone yogi in a cave, meditating for hours. However, if the Ultimate Truth reveals our interconnectedness with all of life, then we are not living our awakening unless we are sharing it.

This is not just about standing on a soapbox and speaking wisdom. Those who are starving or living in war zones or suffering sickness seldom feel ready to sit and listen to a lecture. It is love that is going to make the difference, and loving action that can change the world.

Love is the pure expression of truth.

For some reason, truth and love have often become separated in the spiritual world, yet another form of a split between Shiva (truth) and Shakti (love). If people feel they can sit and speak truth whilst not practising love, then they are rather deluded. The final union needs to occur: we can meditate to recognize truth, but then to be complete we need to learn compassion so that we can express that truth.

So many wars have been fought in the name of religious belief. This is a classic case of what happens when truth and love become separated. If I call truth by one name and you call it by another, then we are ready to go to war. But what value is a truth that kills to defend itself? The ultimate truth is love and needs no defence.

So it seems we urgently need spiritual systems that empower us to unite these apparent opposites. We need the tools to heal situations in which judgement and separation have been formed. We need structures that guide us in forgiveness and heart-opening, and help us to move the energy that has become blocked and distorted. We also need a new state of reverence for the Earth, this planet, the Divine Feminine in her form as Mother Earth. We need to make sure that the enlightenment of the heavens is connected with the enlivenment here on the earth.

Tantra is one such system. There are others, of course. Tantra is not the only one. However, there are many gifts that Tantra has that we need right now.

Having witnessed more than 15 years of transformation in the field of Tantra, I would love to see it serving the world on an even wider level. There are some areas in which I feel Tantra could really give back to the world, and could be integrated into society in various ways, including:

❖ Couples having access to support for their relationships, not only about fixing problems but also for nourishing love, joy and intimacy together.

❖ Education for teenagers that promotes healthy relating and sacred, respectful intimacy and union.

❖ Healing in the area of sexual abuse and rape, working with *both* abusers and victims.

❖ Tools of communication and connection used in areas where there has been gender or racial conflict.

❖ Uniting of personal spiritual practice with practical environmental action.

There are moments in big Tantra events when we are all dancing together or singing together, or we are standing holding hands in a silent circle, and I look around and see a world of love and union.

There is a creative energy that is interconnected between everyone.

I see what happens when deep healing has occurred and projections have been cleared, and there is a love in the air that is tangible.

I see people living truth and sharing that together.

I see that we are all here to wake each other up through our love.

In those moments I feel I have a glimpse of what is possible in the world and of how we could live if we knew it was available.

Loka samasta sukhino bhavantu.
May all beings be happy and free.

Bibliography
and Recommended Reading

Anand, M. *The Art of Sexual Magic* (Jeremy P. Tarcher, 2004): Margot Anand has gathered together practices that involve moving sexual energy with intention to support manifestation and creation.

Chia, M. and Abrams, R. *The Multi-Orgasmic Couple* (HarperOne, 2002): An easy-to-use interpretation of ancient Taoist Sexual Arts, designed for modern couples (there are also two related volumes in the series, one for men and for women).

Douglas, N. and Slinger, P. *Sexual Secrets* (Destiny Books, 1999): A wonderfully illustrated guide to Tantra and Tao, covering aspects of their history and practices.

Edwards, L. *Awakening Kundalini: the Path to Radical Freedom* (Sounds True Inc., 2013): A comprehensive guide to awakening and working with the kundalini energy.

Frawley, D. *Tantric Yoga and the Wisdom Goddesses* (Lotus Press, 1994): Both academic and practical, this book gives a great foundational introduction to Tantric Yoga, especially great for working with the elements and the Goddess energies.

Haas, S. *The Book for Dharma* (Veda Wisdom Books, 2013): A guide to understanding dharma and how to live according to your highest truth.

Long, B. *Making Love* (Barry Long Books, 2004): A discourse on the shifts in perception required to move into a deep and profound form of lovemaking.

Odier, D. *Desire* (Inner Traditions, 2001): Delving in detail into the topic of desire and the Tantric approach. Daniel has an academic background but also teaches in a highly experiential way.

ibid. The Doors of Joy (Watkins Publishing, 2014): A guide to contemplations and meditations for moving into an embodied state of joy based upon Tantric practices.

ibid. Tantric Quest (Inner Traditions, 1997): Odier's own story of his encounter with a Tantrika in India. This is the book I recommend most often to those who want to read about Tantra.

Orford, S. *Tantra, Sex, Orgasm and Meditation* (Live in the Present, 2011): Blends theory about Tantra with a personal story of a Tantric initiation.

Osho, *The Book of Secrets* (Osho Media International, 2012): Osho's discourse on the *Vigyan Bhairav Tantra* is very comprehensive. Being a discourse he talks on many subjects around the topic as well as on the meditations themselves.

Reps, P. *Zen Flesh, Zen Bones.* (Tuttle Publishing, 1957).

Roche, L. *The Radiance Sutras* (Sounds True, Inc., 2014): A beautiful poetic interpretation of the *Vigyan Bhairav Tantra Sutras*.

Sarita, M. A. *Divine Sexuality: The joy of Tantra.* (Findhorn Press, 2011). A very accessible and practical guide for couples to enter Tantric lovemaking.

Schucman, H. *A Course in Miracles* (The Foundation for Inner Peace, 1976): A complete spiritual guide for shifting perception and learning the art of forgiveness.

Shankarananda, S. *Consciousness Is Everything* (Shaktipat Press, 2003): A guide to Kashmiri Shaivism with personal accounts and experiences included.

Shaw, M. *Passionate Enlightenment* (Princeton University Press, 1995): Miranda Shaw is both an academic and a practitioner, who has translated many ancient Tantric texts with a view to clearing out any cultural gender-based bias from the Victorian-era male translators. Endorsed by the Dalai Lama.

Stiles, M. *Tantra Yoga Secrets* (Weiser Books, 2011): A guide to moving through the 18 levels of Tantric yoga practice.

Tigunait, P. *Tantra Unveiled* (Himalayan Institute Press, 1999): Born and raised in a traditional Tantric culture Tigunait provides an accessible description of classical Tantra.

Wallis, C. *Tantra Illuminated* (Mattamayura Press, 2013): A well-researched, academic yet accessible review of Tantra, focusing on Kashmiri Shaivism.

Yogani, *Tantra* (AYP Publishing, 2006): A clear and easy-to-use guide to Tantric yoga and practices.

Resources

Shashi Solluna

Shashi Solluna offers online courses – including teacher training, see below, meditations, articles and other online material at ShashiSolluna.com.

Many meditations from this book can be found at: ShashiSolluna.com/Tantric-Tools

Platforms

LiveTantra is a platform of trustworthy Tantra teachers contributing articles, videos and online courses. For more information visit www.livetantra.com

Tantra schools

The following list of schools includes those where I have personally studied; however, there are many more worldwide, and I suggest letting recommendations and testimonials be your guide to finding the right one for you.

Agama Yoga

Led by Swami Vivekananda, this is an international school based in Thailand offering training in Tantric yoga, Tantra theory and meditation.

Daniel Odier School

Transmission of practices from Tantrika Lalita Devi. Daniel also gives discourses and teaches the Tandava practice.

Embodied Intimacy

Led by David Cates, this school focuses on the 'belly to belly' practice, in which participants drop in deeply to this present moment.

Five Element Dance

Daisy Kaye (student and co-teacher with Shashi Solluna) offers training in the five elements through dance, touch and meditation.

Mystical Dance

Monika Nataraj offers courses in sacred dance and Tantra for women.

Paths of Transformation

John Hawken leads explorations into Tantra: massage and dark eros, blended with a shamanic flavour.

School for Kundalini Yoga

Founded by Yogi Bajan, this worldwide yoga school offers Tantric yoga and meditation for White Tantra. You won't find anything sexual here, but incredible techniques for working with sexual energy and attaining high levels of consciousness.

Skydancing Tantra
Margot Anand offers a blend of classical Tantra and Neo-Tantra, psychological and sexual healing with meditations and practices.

Tao Tantric Arts
Led by Shashi Solluna and Minke de Vos this training fuses Taoist sexual arts and Tantra methods – the space is very safe and focused on energy.

Tantra Essence
Ma Sarita offers training for couples and individuals in a safe and sacred space.

Universal Healing Tao
Leading author on Taoist practices, Grand-Master Mantak Chia, focuses on energy movement using qigong with sexual arts as one segment of the whole curriculum.

ABOUT THE AUTHOR

Shashi Solluna has a BA (Oxon) degree in Experimental Psychology and has been immersed in the field of Tantra since the millennium. Her adult life has been dedicated to the spiritual path, and she has lived in India, Thailand and Bali for many years. As a manager of a busy retreat centre, Shashi was able to invite teachers from all over the world, thus she was able to learn from many great sources.

Shashi trained residentially for several years with Grandmaster Mantak Chia in the arts of Taoism. She lived at the Osho 'ashram' in Pune, India, for several years, discovering the Osho Tantra lineage. Shashi also trained as a Tantra Instructor with Agama Yoga, a path of classical tantric practice, Kashmiri Shaivism and tantric yoga. She now weaves together the wisdom and practices of these different strands of Tantra in her own work.

Shashi's passion is to create experiences in which energy can awaken back to its true nature, taking us home to our truth in a fully embodied way. She teaches globally at Tantra festivals and seminars, as well as running her own month-long teacher-training programmes. She has also produced a feature-length documentary following one man's journey through Tantra, called *Sex to Spirit*. In the future, she would like to see tantric wisdom reaching our teenagers and youth to help guide them into healthy, loving forms of intimacy.

www.shashisolluna.com

HAY HOUSE

Look within

Join the conversation about latest products,
events, exclusive offers and more.

 Hay House UK

 @HayHouseUK

 @hayhouseuk

 healyourlife.com

We'd love to hear from you!